THE INFERENCE
THAT MAKES SCIENCE

THE AQUINAS LECTURE, 1992

THE INFERENCE
THAT MAKES SCIENCE

ERNAN McMULLIN

MARQUETTE
UNIVERSITY
PRESS

Library of Congress Catalog Card Number: 92-80351

ISBN 0-87462-159-3

Marquette University Press

Second Printing 1995

Printed in the United States of America

MARQUETTE UNIVERSITY PRESS
MILWAUKEE

The Association of Jesuit University Presses

Prefatory

The Wisconsin-Alpha Chapter of Phi Sigma Tau, the National Honor Society for Philosophy at Marquette University, each year invites a scholar to deliver a lecture in honor of St. Thomas Aquinas.

The 1992 Aquinas Lecture, *The Inference That Makes Science*, was delivered in the Tony and Lucille Weasler Auditorium on Sunday, March 1, 1992, by Ernan McMullin, Professor of Philosophy at the University of Notre Dame, where he holds the John Cardinal O'Hara Chair of Philosophy and is Director of the Program in History and Philosophy of Science.

Professor McMullin earned a B.Sc. in Physics and a B.D. in theology at Maynooth College, Ireland. He held a fellowship in theoretical physics at the Dublin Institute for Advanced Studies in 1949-1950 and earned a Ph.D. in philosophy at the University of Louvain. He began teaching at Notre Dame in 1954 and became full professor in 1967. He has been visiting professor at the University of Minnesota, the University of Cape Town, and at the University of California, Los Angeles.

His books include *The Concept of Matter* (1963), *Galileo, Man of Science* (1967), *Newton on Matter and Activity* (1978), *The Concept of Matter in Modern Philosophy* (1978), *Death and Decision* (1978), *Evolution and Creation* (1985), *Con-

struction and Constraint: The Shaping of Scientific Rationality (1988), and *Rationality, Realism, and the Growth of Knowledge*, which will appear soon.

He has also written over two hundred journal articles, chapters in books, encyclopedia entries, and other scholarly pieces on a wide variety of topics in philosophy and in the history and philosophy of science.

Professor McMullin is a fellow of the American Academy of Arts and Sciences, a fellow of the International Academy of the History of Science, and a fellow of the American Association for the Advancement of Science. He was awarded the Aquinas Medal in 1981 by the American Catholic Philosophical Association and has received honorary doctorates from Loyola University of Chicago and from the National University of Ireland. He has served as president of the American Philosophical Association, Western Division, of the Philosophy of Science Association, of the Metaphysical Society of America, and of the American Catholic Philosophical Association.

To Professor McMullin's distinguished list of publications, Phi Sigma Tau is pleased to add: *The Inference That Makes Science*.

THE INFERENCE
THAT MAKES SCIENCE

by

ERNAN MCMULLIN

Contents

THE INFERENCE
THAT MAKES SCIENCE

Is there a pattern of inference that particularly characterizes the sciences of nature? Theorists of science, from Aristotle's day to our own, have on the whole tended to answer in the affirmative, though views have changed as to what that pattern is. It has usually been linked, in one way or another, with *explanation*. To demonstrate in proper scientific form, Aristotle noted, is also to explain. The credibility of a theoretical inference, it might be said today, is proportionate to its explanatory success.

My aim in this essay is to pursue this theme, the nature of the inference that constitutes a claim as "science", both on a historical and a systematic level. As historians, we shall find a continuity of concern, a link across the ages that separate the Greek inquiry into nature from our own vastly more complex scientific enterprise. But we shall also discover discontinuity, the abandonment of earlier ideals as unworkable. Indeed, it is arguable that the failure (in its own terms) of Aristotelian natural philosophy may to some degree have been linked with its emphasis on demonstration, on a science of nature that would rest on causal claims held to be evident in their own right. We shall find a worry among medieval Aristotelians that a demonstrative science of nature might be very difficult of achievement or might even be out of reach. The deep shift that we have come to call the "Scientific Revolution" can be regarded as in large part an attempt to construct an alternative to demonstration, a "New Organon", as its most influential protagonist dubbed it. We shall discover that the New Organon was fundamentally ambiguous, that it involved two quite different patterns of inference. It took more than two centuries before this was finally recognized. And even in our own century, it was implicitly denied, first by the logical positivists, and more recently by those who, for whatever reason, reject scientific realism. Since our canvas is such a large one, we shall have to be content with broad strokes. Besides Aristotle, there will be a host of other characters: Grosseteste, Zabarella, Bacon, Whewell, Peirce.... And Aquinas, needless to say, will not be forgotten.

We shall come to see that the natural sciences involve many types of inference-pattern; three of these interlock in a special way to produce what we shall call retroductive inference, the kind of complex inference that supports causal theory. Since theories are primarily designed to *explain*, explanatory power obviously plays a major part in their warranting. But there is a good deal of disagreement about how this warranting role may best be understood. We shall, for example, challenge the thesis often associated with the hypothetico-deductive (H-D) account of scientific knowledge which would limit the warrant of a theory to the sum of the verified consequences deductively derivable from it.

It may be worth noting from the beginning that the attempt to define "the inference that makes science" is not intended to furnish a criterion of demarcation between science and non-science. The issue of demarcation has been actively debated ever since Popper made it central to his philosophy of science. We shall not address it here. Suffice it to say that retroductive inference makes use of ingredients that are commonplace in human reasoning generally. One finds them in any inquiry into causes, in the work of a detective or a newspaper reporter, for example. What is distinctive about the way in which explanatory theories are constructed and tested in natural science is the precision, as well as the explicitness, with which retroductive inference is deployed. But this alone is not enough to enable a sharp boundary line to be drawn. There will be large areas where a clear-cut decision will not be possible, where, for example, the questions: "good science or bad science?" and "science or non-science?" will inevitably overlap.

The sciences of human behavior pose a further, and equally debatable, question. Is the pattern of inference that constitutes these as "science" the same as (or, at least, very similar to) that employed by the natural sciences? Do they explain in more or less the sense in which, say, chemistry explains? Do they work back from observed effects to underlying structural causes as chemical theories do? Once again, we shall have to set aside an important issue in order to focus on the already-large one at hand. Our concern here is with the natural sciences, and with a single question: in what kind of complex inference do they (ideally) culminate? Of course, this limitation would have been foreign to the intentions of Aristotle, from whose seminal work on the theory of science, the *Posterior Analytics*, our inquiry takes its start. His aim was to discover what the ideal of knowledge (*episteme*) should be, while warning against seeking a greater degree of precision in any domain than the nature of the inquiry admits.

Part One: Demonstration Alone

Aristotle on demonstration: What makes knowledge "scientific" (*epistemonikos*) according to Aristotle is that it should constitute strict demonstration (*apodeixis*). And by demonstration he means an inference from premisses which are true, primary, immediate, more knowable (*gnorimos*) than, and prior to the conclusion, and further that the premisses furnish an *explanation* of the conclusion.[1] It is not enough that the inference be a deductively valid syllogism; logical validity does not suffice to render a piece of reasoning scientific. It is not even enough that the inference be a valid one from true premisses. The premisses must be of a quite definite kind, and they must specify in a unique way the cause of the effect or property of which scientific knowledge is desired.

How are the premisses of the requisite sort to be obtained? Not by further demonstration, for that would lead to regress. The premisses must be primary and immediate; that is, they must carry conviction in their *own* right once they are properly understood. (The English term 'self-evident', with its overtone of 'obvious', can be misleading in this context.) But how is such an understanding to be attained? Aristotle knew perfectly well that on an answer to this question his entire account of science would stand or fall. But he is famously laconic in his response.[2]

Experience (*empeiria*) is, it appears, crucial to the discovery of the necessary premisses, the starting-points of demonstration in natural science:

It pertains to experience to provide the principles of any subject. In astronomy, for example, astronomical experience supplied the principles of the science; it was only when the phenomena were adequately grasped that the demonstrations proper to astronomy were discovered. Similarly with any other art or science.[3]

Through perception we register particulars, but these particulars themselves are not objects of scientific knowledge, which is directed to universals.[4] The process leading from the perception of particular things to the grasp of universals Aristotle calls *epagoge*, which is often translated as 'induction'. Is there, then, a second sort of inference, a form of systematic generalization, that provides the starting-point for demonstration? Ought we say that Aristotle proposes not one but two forms of inference, demonstration and induction, together leading to science (*episteme*)? *Epagoge* is, indeed, sometimes described as though it proceeded by enumeration, or depended on a systematic comparison of instances.[5]

But any resemblance to what Bacon will later call induction is misleading. In Aristotle's view, it seems, rather, to be a process of *recognizing* the universal in a few particulars, of grasping the phenomena as instances of a specific universal. It does not depend on sample size.[6] There is first the ability to perceive (which humans share with animals); the perceptions persist and constitute memory. And "out of frequently repeated memories of the same thing develops experience".[7] In this way the universal is, as it were, "stabilized" in the soul, bringing about a state of mind called *nous* (insight, intuition, comprehension). *Nous* is a direct grasp of the universals already implicit in perception, and is brought about by *epagoge*.[8] It is more basic than demonstration; it is, Aristotle assures us, the originative source of science since it anchors the premisses from which demonstration begins.[9]

Underlying this analysis, of course, is Aristotle's doctrine of the mind's ability to receive the form of an object. "The thinking part of the soul must therefore be, while impassible, capable of receiving the form of an object; that is, it must be potentially identical in character with its object without being the object".[10] So that "mind is what it is in virtue of becoming all things".[11] The veridical character of *episteme* depends on this ability of mind to grasp form, as presented in perceived appearance. The form conveys the essential nature of the thing perceived, and so the basic premisses of demonstration can be required not only to be true but to be necessarily true, displaying causal relationships that are "more knowable" in themselves than the fact to be demonstrated.

Here in brief and familiar outline is how Aristotle proposes that science should be acquired. There are obviously many difficulties and obscurities in the account. How, for example, is one to deal with the obvious problem of sense-error? Aristotle himself points it out: "We must maintain that not everything which appears is true; firstly, because even if sensation... is not false, still appearance is not the same as sensation".[12] Only *"reliable"* (*aei kurios*) phenomena can serve as a basis for natural science, he reminds his reader.[13] But how is one to know, in an absolutely assured way, which of the phenomena can be counted as reliable?

More fundamentally, what justifies us in supposing that the forms given us in perception really *do* convey the essence of the thing perceived? Aristotle recognizes in passing that there may be a "failure" in perception when we are unable to perceive the inner structures of a substance on which a property, like the ability of a burning-glass to set objects on fire, may depend.[14] If we *were* to be able to see pores in the glass and the light passing through these pores, then "the reason of the kindling would be clear to us". But as it is, such microstructures lie permanently outside the range of our senses. "Light shines through a lantern because that which consists of relatively small particles necessarily passes through pores larger than those particles".[15] Aristotle is clearly aware of the challenge this sort of explanation poses for his phenomenalist account of the natural sciences, but he nowhere deals with this directly.[16] Instead, he restricts himself to observed correlations in the examples on which he relies (as in his celebrated explanation of the lack of incisors in the upper jaws of horned animals in terms of the nutriment needed for their horns[17]), or to simple causal analyses, as in his frequent references to eclipses.

In a significant passage, he draws a distinction between knowledge "of the fact" (*oti, quia*) and knowledge "of the reasoned fact" (*dioti, propter quid*). Since he is trying in this passage to explain how demonstration works, the examples he chooses are of special interest. They are drawn from astronomy, an odd choice it might seem. Our perceptual knowledge of the heavenly bodies is obviously very limited; they are, he notes elsewhere:

> excellent beyond compare and divine, but less accessible to knowledge. The evidence that might throw light on them, and on the problems we long to solve respecting them, is furnished but scantily by sensation. Whereas respecting perishable plants and animals we have abundant information, living as we do in their midst. Both domains,

however, have their special charm. The scanty conceptions to which we can attain of celestial things give us, from their excellence, more pleasure then all our knowledge of the world in which we live. . . . On the other hand, in certitude and completeness our knowledge of terrestrial things has the advantage. Moreover, their greater nearness and affinity to us balances somewhat the loftier interest of the heavenly things. . . .[18]

Where the presumptive pores in glass that allow light to pass are imperceptible to us because of their minute size, the difficulty with the heavenly bodies is one both of distance and of nature. Not only does their great distance prevent us from observing their properties in any other than a perfunctory way, but (in Aristotle's view, at least) we have reason to believe that these bodies are fundamentally different in nature to the bodies of earth by means of which our perceptual expectations have been molded. So our explorations of the skies must be regarded as conjectural. Why, then, choose examples drawn from astronomy to illustrate a thesis about strict demonstration in natural science? Was it just because of his general fondness for astronomical illustrations ("a half-glimpse of persons that we love is more delightful than a more leisurely look at others"[19]), or was it because these examples were in some special way apposite?

The non-twinkling planets: The distinction he draws between two grades of knowledge was intended in part to help overcome the difficulty of discovering a unique causal explanation when one has to work backwards from perceived effect to less familiar cause. To see this will require a detailed analysis of the key passage in the *Posterior Analytics* (I, 13). He gives two examples of the sort of problem that, despite appearances, lends itself to demonstration. The most striking property of the planets (other than the "wandering" motion that gave them their original Greek name) is that they do not twinkle. Alone among the heavenly bodies they shine with a steady light. How are we to explain this? How are we to "demonstrate" the property of non-twinkling they possess? Only by finding the more basic property of planets responsible for the fact that they do not twinkle. Aristotle proposes nearness as a plausible candidate. But *are* the planets nearer than the other heavenly bodies? A confident assertion follows: "That which does not twinkle is near: we must take this truth as having been reached by induction or sense-perception".[20]

This gives him an apparent proof of nearness:

S1 A   That which does not twinkle is near
   B   The planets do not twinkle
       Therefore the planets are near

This he calls a demonstration of the fact (*oti*). It is an improper demonstration because it is not causally explanatory: non-twinkling does not *explain* the nearness. The major premiss is merely an observed correlation between two properties of shining bodies: if they do not twinkle, then they are observed to be near. This is sufficient, however, to prove the truth of the conclusion. And now this conclusion can become the minor premiss of a new syllogism:

S2 A   Nearby (shining) objects do not twinkle
   B   Planets are near
       Therefore planets do not twinkle

This is (Aristotle says) a demonstration of the reasoned fact, a proper demonstration, because it gives the cause of (or reason for) the fact. The middle term joining the extremes functions to *explain* the link between them: nearness is the reason why planets do not twinkle. What gives this demonstration force *as* demonstration for Aristotle is not merely its syllogistic validity but its explanatory force.

But *is* S2 a proper demonstration? It would appear not, and for two separate reasons. Neither premiss seems to qualify as the sort of necessary truth that a demonstration requires as starting-point. How would one establish the *necessity* of S2A, the claim that nearby shining objects do not twinkle? It is not enough that it just happens to be true (if indeed it *is* true). "True in every instance", Aristotle himself reminds us, does not suffice; the attribute (non-twinkling, in this case) must be "commensurately universal", that is, it must belong to every instance (of nearby shining object) *essentially*.[21] It must be shown to "inhere necessarily in the subject". Induction-as-generalization will not do; at best, all it can show is factual correlation of attribute and subject. *Epagoge* cannot (as Aristotle knows) reduce to induction, in the sense of generalization.

It is worth noting, indeed emphasizing, that exactly the same issue arose for the logical positivists when they tried to define the notion of "law" that was so basic to their account of explanation. It is not enough for an inductive generalization to be *factually* true ("everyone in this room is over five feet tall") for it to serve as the starting-point of a scientific explanation. An "accidental" universal will not sustain the sort of counterfactual conditional ("if x had been in this room. . .") that is taken to be diagnostic of "genuine" (what Aristotle would call "essential") lawlikeness. We shall return to this later. Suffice for the moment to say that any account of science that rests (as Aristotle's does) on attributes given in perception is bound to have trouble in separating "essential" from accidental linkages, in construing causality as anything more than invariable correlation.

How is *epagoge* supposed to lead us to the insight that nearness is the cause of non-twinkling in the planets? Is some kind of immediate grasp of the universals, nearness and non-twinkling (in the case of planets), sufficient? It is clearly not enough for *epagoge* to bring us to recognize the two universals in their particular instances; they have also to be seen as causally (necessarily) related. In *On the Heavens*, Aristotle does give a hint as to what the causal relationship might be. Noting that the sun appears to twinkle at sunrise and sunset, he goes on:

> This appearance is due not to the sun itself but to the distance from which we observe it. The visual ray being excessively prolonged becomes weak and wavering. The same reason probably accounts for the apparent twinkling of the fixed stars and the absence of twinkling in the planets. The planets are near, so that the visual ray reaches them in its full vigor, but when it

comes to the fixed stars it is quivering
because of the distance and its excessive
extension; and its tremor produces an
appearance of motion in the star.[22]

Here is a *theoretical* account of why twinkling
occurs, and how it may be due to distance. It
relies on the notion of a "visual ray" that goes out
from the eye, and is attenuated by distance. This is
obviously not something that could be derived
directly by *epagoge* from perception of particulars.
It is a tentative conjecture about an underlying
process that might account for the twinkling of the
distant stars. Its explanatory force comes from its
ampliative character: it does not just associate
twinkling with great distance, but suggests why
this association might betoken a causal connection. The necessity is of a weak hypothetical
sort: *if* there are visual rays and *if* visual rays tend
to attenuate with distance (more theory needed
here), then the stars will (necessarily) twinkle.
What allows one to transcend mere factual correlation in this case is not *nous* as direct insight into
essence, into causal relations themselves not given
in perception, but plausible theoretical recon-
struction in terms of postulated underlying structures.

In his "official" account of the nature of
demonstration in natural science in the *Posterior
Analytics*, Aristotle nowhere explicitly admits the

mediating role played by theory in the establishing of causal connections. He leaves the reader to believe that there is a power of mind which can somehow, subsequent to perception, attain to the essence of natural things immediately. It is not hard to see why he does this. It is crucial, in his mind, that the premisses from which science begins be "primary", that is, not themselves in need of further evidential support. They must be *definitively* true. Unless this be granted, there is no hope of attaining the "eternal and necessary knowledge" that he holds out as the aim of his inquiry into nature. But once one admits that either premiss is "theoretical" in the sense sketched above, one has implicitly given up on this aim. For theory (e.g., about visual rays) is clearly not primary; it is in need of further corroboration, of systematic testing. Nor is it definitive; Aristotle himself allows that his suggestion that visual rays attenuate in vigor the further they travel is at best only probable.

His attempt to supplement the phenomenalism of his starting-point with an optimistic rationalist account of what *epagoge* can accomplish, brings out the main weakness in his account of demonstration. This can be seen in another way if we shift attention to the minor premiss, S2B. How are we to know that this premiss is *true*? Perception alone does not allow us to claim that the planets are near. Their nearness is not perceived; it has to be inferred. How, then, can the minor premiss be regarded as primary? Aristotle introduces a distinction between something "more knowable in itself" and something "more knowable to us".[23] The fact that planets do not twinkle is more knowable to us; the fact that they are near is more knowable in itself because it serves as a causal principle. But how do we get from the former to the latter?

S1 makes use of that which we know (that the planets do not twinkle) to arrive at a new truth: that the planets are near. The order of exposition followed by Aristotle suggests that the "demonstration of the fact" provides the needed minor premiss (S2B) for the demonstration proper displayed in S2. Does this work? Everything depends on the major premiss S1A: That which does not twinkle is near. This is where the choice of the non-twinkling planets turns out to be a brilliant one. For one can plausibly point the causal arrow in either direction. Distance causes twinkling (which yields S1A, if one allows the negation of the rather vague term 'distant' to be equivalent to 'near'). Perhaps this is why Aristotle says so confidently of S1A: "We must take this truth as having been reached by *epagoge* or by perception".[24] (As we have already seen, however, something more than generalization is required here, something like the attenuation theory of *On the Heavens*.) If one grants that (great) distance "causes" twinkling, then the (relative) nearness of the planets is established. But Aristotle clearly takes the causal arrow to operate in the other direction also: nearness causes (explains) non-twinkling (S2A). This is much more problematic. Distance is, so far as one can see, not the only possible cause of the twinkle in starlight. So nearness alone does not *demonstratively* explain why the planets do not twinkle. This latter is not a deductive causal relationship, though Aristotle's choice of negative characteristics (non-distant, non-twinkling) that can be thought of in a positive way (nearness, emitting steady light) conceals this. The causal arrow does not really point in both directions here, though it would be easy to miss this.

Aristotle was too good a logician not to realize what was going on here. He recognizes that a condition is necessary in order for his analysis of proper and improper demonstration to hold. The two attributes (non-twinkling and nearness in the case of the planets) have to be reciprocally predicable, or to put this in another way, the major premiss has to be convertible. Whatever does not twinkle is near, *and* whatever is near does not twinkle. This is equivalent to requiring that the cause postulated be the only *possible* cause, so that one can infer in either direction.

Now, of course, if this can be taken for granted, the problem of constructing a demonstration is greatly eased. There is still the question of how *epagoge* is to lead us to the grasp of causal relationships. But at least we do not have the further problem of dealing with alternative possible causes, each of them sufficient to explain the effect. The normally hypothetical character of inference from effect back to efficient cause (what we shall later call retroductive inference) has been tacitly suppressed.

A glance at Aristotle's other illustration of the two kinds of demonstration bears this out:

S3 A Whatever waxes thus is spherical
   B The moon waxes thus
      Therefore the moon is spherical

This is demonstration of the fact that the moon is spherical, relying on the knowledge that the moon goes through certain phases in relation to the sun's position, and, second, that waxing in this way implies a spherical shape.

S4 A Whatever is spherical waxes thus
   B The moon is spherical
      Therefore the moon waxes thus

This is demonstration proper because the spherical shape is the cause of the waxing, and the truth of the minor premiss (S4B) is certified in advance by S3. Aristotle remarks that a "quick wit" (*agkinoia*) is needed in order to grasp that the lunar phases are due to a reflection of sunlight.[25] But this is a case where the perceived phenomenal correlation leads particularly easily to a postulation of the causal connection. The wit does not have to be especially quick!

More important, the major premiss once again looks more or less convertible: spherical shape causes waxing thus, and waxing thus (more or less) implies a spherical shape. It is true that other possible causes of the waxing could not have been entirely ruled out in Aristotle's day, but it would have seemed overwhelmingly likely that sunlight falling on a spherical moon was the cause. Geometrical optics lends itself nicely to necessary-seeming claims and to simple inductive evidence. Thus, not only do we have a cause but it can plausibly be represented as the only *possible* cause. And this is needed for Aristotle's account of demonstration to work. Such cases are obviously not typical of the broad range of contexts in natural science where demonstration/explanation is sought. And even these special cases do not really enable necessity to be claimed for the premisses. The transition from "better known to us" to "more knowable in itself" must remain tentative except in the most favorable of cases. Talk about the "pores" that allow light to pass through glass, of "visual rays" and the way they are attenuated over distance, of the manner in which nutrients that would otherwise have been channeled to the incisors of the upper jaw are diverted to the production of horns in horned animals, cannot be fitted into the straitjacket of demonstration. Strict demonstration in cases such as the astronomical ones above will work only when a causal relationship between A and B can be "seen" to hold with necessity, and when B also requires A, i.e., when A can be "seen" to be the only *possible* cause of B.

The living world: This latter condition would be particularly difficult to satisfy in the domain of living things, the domain to which Aristotle devoted such an extraordinary effort. It has often been noted that in his voluminous writings on animals there are few, if any, instances of the demonstrative form laid down in the **Posterior Analytics**. This has, indeed, furnished a major topic of scholarly research in recent years.[26] In his review of more than five hundred animal species, he lists for each species numerous properties that could serve as *differentiae*. Scholars have tried hard to extract a natural classification from this profusion, but it is clear that none is there. Further, it seems doubtful that one was intended, since the divisions given are frequently criss-cross, as Aristotle himself notes.[27] He does suggest possible causal connections between properties: the lungs temper the heat of the body in warm-blooded animals;[28] the kidneys carry more fat than do other internal organs because the kidneys require a greater supply of heat, being closer to the surface and having much "concoction" to perform, and fat is a cause of heat.[29]

From our point of view, these would seem to be no more than causal speculations, prompted by some fairly casual correlations and some very general theories about the role of such causal agencies as heat and fat in the animal body. How could they ever be made demonstrative? What would the "primary premisses" in the study of living things look like?[30] Functional explanations of the sort Aristotle relied on offer a particular challenge in that regard: "The function of the lungs is to cool the blood and hence the body." Even if one could show that respiration is needed to cool the body and that it *does* cool the body, how would one show that it does not also have another function? This is the equivalent of the problem about the convertibility of the major premiss in the case of the astronomical examples earlier. What he needs, according to his theory of demonstration, is definitions in which the essences of the various natural kinds are expressed. But if these definitions are complex, containing a list of *differentiae* (as he appears to envisage), and if many of the terms used are equivocal, "said in many ways", as he admits they are, how could one ever trace a unique causal line with necessity from the *genus* or from one or a cluster of the *differentiae* to the property to be explained? The case to which later Aristotelians would always return was that of man, with a conveniently simple single *differentia*. But this, as Aristotle himself recognized, was altogether untypical of the inquiry into animal natures generally. "If demonstration still remained an ideal in zoology, as in mathematics, it was an ideal that had to recede the more Aristotle's zoological researches progressed."[31] To what extent was Aristotle himself aware of the limited applicability of his teaching on demonstration?

Introducing an ingenious but highly speculative account of comets, shooting stars, and the "fuel" that sustains them, he says: "We consider a satisfactory explanation of phenomena inaccessible to observation to have been given when our account of them is free of impossibilities".[32] A weak criterion, indeed, in comparison with the exacting demands of demonstration! In *On the Heavens*, he frequently laments how far short of demonstration his account falls: "When anyone shall succeed in finding proofs of greater precision, gratitude will be due to him for the discovery, but at present we must be content with what seems to be the case".[33] He obviously thought that proofs "of greater precision" were, in principle, constructible; the significance to his doctrine of *epagoge* of "phenomena inaccessible to observation" had not, to all appearances, sunk in. Our later story will be devoted to the reweaving of these threads that he for the first time separated off. The patterns of inference/explanation in contemporary science are strikingly different from those proposed in the *Posterior Analytics*. But the quest for a causal explanation of natural phenomena that should be as epistemically secure as possible still remains.

Part Two: Enlarging Demonstration

It would take us too far afield to comment on the medieval discussions of the nature of demonstration in the detail they deserve. Our main goal in this essay is to analyze the three primary patterns that have been proposed over the years for explanation/inference in natural science. We have already seen one of these, and must rather summarily move on to the other two. But it is worth asking first about the extent to which the transition to other inference-patterns was already under way among medieval writers on the nature of science. To what extent did medieval commentators on the *Posterior Analytics* show an awareness of the difficulties involved in finding "commensu-

rately universal" relationships, the only kind yielding demonstration proper? Did they, for example,
relax the demand for premisses that would be
seen to be not only true but *necessarily* true, once
properly understood? Did they take steps to sys-
tematize the process involved in *epagoge* in order
to ensure that the regularities discovered in nature
would be genuinely universal ones? We shall see
that on the whole the requirements of strict
demonstration were not relaxed, but that significant efforts were made to grapple with the problems that these requirements imposed. We shall
also see that some contemporary attempts to con-
strue medieval enlargements of the doctrine of
demonstration as actively preparing the way for
modern accounts of scientific method are, though
laudable in the generosity of their intention, con-
siderably overstated.

Looking at the Middle Ages as a whole, one
would obviously have to separate two quite diverse
methodological traditions, the Aristotelian and the
nominalist. And one would have to bear in mind
the great diversity within both of those traditions
themselves. The Aristotelians remained faithful,
on the whole, to the ideal of demonstration set
down in the *Posterior Analytics*, while developing
some aspects of that doctrine, the distinction
between demonstrations *propter quid* and *quia*, for
example, much more fully than Aristotle had

done. The nominalists began to shape the notion of inductive generalization, entirely rejecting the notion of necessary connection between essence and property on which the older notion of demonstration had been based. The idea of causal explanation as tentative and "consequential", resting in large part, that is, on the verified observational consequences drawn from it, only sporadically made its appearance and, among Aristotelians, never as any other than a stage on the way to demonstration proper. In lieu of a detailed historical treatment, we shall pick out for brief comment three of the leading representatives of the tradition of the *Posterior Analytics*, Grosseteste, Aquinas, and Zabarella, each of whom has a special interest for our story.

Grosseteste: Forty   years   ago,   Alistair Crombie in a widely-discussed book declared that:

> As a result of their attempts to answer the Greek question: How is it possible to reach with the greatest possible certainty true premisses for demonstrated knowledge of the world of experience? the natural philosophers of Latin Christendom in the thirteenth and fourteenth centuries created the experimental science characteristic of modern times.[34]

This was the "continuity thesis", announced earlier by the historian/philosopher of science, Pierre Duhem, now proposed in its strongest possible form. More specifically, Crombie claimed that the appearance of Robert Grosseteste's commentary on the *Posterior Analytics* (c. 1225), which made that difficult work accessible for the first time to Latin readers,[35] in conjunction with Grosseteste's own works on optics and other scientific topics, initiated a new approach to natural science. Grosseteste's distinctive contribution was "to emphasize the importance of *falsification* in the search for true causes and to develop the method of verification and falsification into a systematic method of experimental procedure".[36]

Later historians of the period have, on the whole, been unsympathetic to this reading of Grosseteste. In a recent study of that philosopher's work, James McEvoy writes:

> If a broadly adequate methodology be regarded as a necessary and quasi-sufficient basis for scientific advance, then it becomes at once essential and embarrassingly difficult to account for the relative scientific sterility of the late medieval and early Renaissance period, if one grants – and this is the force of Crombie's main thesis – that the requisite methodology was already available from around 1240 onwards.[37]

To assess the force of this objection to Crombie's thesis, one would have to distinguish between *methodology*, understood in terms of practical prescriptions regarding working procedure, and *conception of science*, taken to specify the sort of knowledge-claim that counts as science proper. Crombie was, of course, claiming originality for Grosseteste and his successors on both scores. It is only the second, his conception of science, that concerns us here. Being right about one's conception of science does not *necessarily* translate into practical success in one's scientific work. Likewise, failure in the latter regard does not necessarily connote failure in the former, so we have to look at the matter more carefully. *Did* Grosseteste transform the Aristotelian notion of demonstration into something akin to the modern idea of experiment-based theoretical inference?

To begin with, he certainly *did* stress the importance of experience as the basis for scientific knowledge, even more perhaps than Aristotle had done.[38] His motive for this, it should be noted, was in large part theological. Because of sin, man's higher powers were corrupted but the humbler power of perception, by standing firm in the rout, enabled the higher powers to recover their proper function of apprehending the essences of things.[39] In practice, the features of the *Posterior Analytics* that he chooses to dwell on are often the empir-

ical examples that Aristotle uses to such good
effect. For example, when discussing the non-
twinkling of the planets, he produces his own
explanation for the twinkling of starlight: the
greater the distance of any object from us, he suggests, the smaller the angle it subtends at the eye
and thus the greater the strain on vision. This
strain and the tremor it induces in the *virtus visiva*
that goes out from the eye to the object causes the
appearance of twinkling.[40] When he discusses, at
considerable length, the connections between lack
of incisors and possession of multiple stomachs in
horned animals, he simply brings together what
Aristotle and some of his later commentators, like
Themistius, have to say in different contexts about
this topic.[41] There is no new observation involved,
and Grosseteste almost certainly had not himself
seen all of the animals mentioned. He does, however, draw attention to a consequence that Aristotle had left unstated: though all horned animals
lack upper incisors, not all those that lack upper
incisors possess horns (camels and hinds, for
example). Thus the properties are not mutually
implicative, or to put this in the traditional way,
the major premiss in any attempted demonstration
of a causal relation between the properties would
not be convertible. In cases like that of the camel,
Grosseteste adds (again following Aristotle), the
animals have other means of defence so that horns

are not needed. (This leaves the camel's lack of upper incisors unexplained; Aristotle and Grosseteste try to make do with a teleological explanation for this by noting that the camel's hard palate substitutes for the lack of incisors.)

Had Grosseteste been of a mind to challenge or revise Aristotle's account of demonstration, this would have been an obvious context in which to do so. Another context would have been where he comments on a particularly difficult passage (II, 16 and 17) in the *Posterior Analytics*, and asks whether the same effect might not be known from experience to be explainable in terms of several different possible causes.[42] Again, he forbears. The most illuminating contexts are those in which he discusses different "opinions" regarding the explanation of specific phenomena. Here one does find him suggesting that the "opinions" may be tested by seeing whether inferences drawn from them conflict with observation or general principle. Crombie draws attention to two such examples, in particular.

In one, Grosseteste reviews four "opinions" regarding the nature of comets and rejects all four of them on the grounds that their consequences are at odds with observation, as well as with "the principles of the special sciences".[43] He advances a fifth view on his own account: a comet is a fire of a transformed non-terrestrial sort linked to its present star or planet by an attraction akin to that between magnet and iron. Though the theory seems fanciful from our perspective, it is governed by the insight that comets share in the revolutions of the heavenly bodies and hence cannot be of a simply terrestrial nature. In another passage, he gives an example to illustrate how the universal is reached by the mind through "the ministry of the senses". The taking of scammony (a purgative widely used in the ancient Greek world) is commonly accompanied by the discharge of red bile.[44] Is the former the cause of the latter? We cannot see such a causal relation directly. But "frequent observation" of the two events as co-occurring leads us to suspect (*estimare*) a third factor which is itself not observable, that is, a causal relation between the two. The power of reason (*ratio*) then comes into play and suggests, by way of test, that scammony should be administered when all other (known) causes of red bile have been excluded from operating. If there is still a discharge of red bile in such cases, "a universal is formed in the reason" affirming the causal connection between the two sorts of occurrence, thus giving rise to a "universal experiential principle".

Though Crombie may have been over-enthusiastic in his original formulation of the continuity thesis, he was surely right to take passages such as these to presage a manner of reasoning in

science that differs fundamentally from demonstration. But the extent of the change is by no
means clear, as the last example shows. Scientific
inquiry still terminates in the reason's directly
grasping a universal causal connection between
the administration of scammony and the discharge
of red bile. Does this claim to understanding con-
tinue to rest on the adequacy of the inductive procedures followed, the exclusion of other relevant
causal factors and the testing of the invariability of
the alleged correlation? In this case, how are we
to know that the connection between the two
kinds of occurrence is of an *essential* nature? Or,
on the other hand, are we to suppose that the
grasp of the causal connection becomes at this
point a direct intuitive one, given that one has now
an adequate familiarity with the concepts
involved? These are the alternatives that faced
Grosseteste and his successors in one guise or
another. He did not himself, so far as one can discover from the texts, resolve in favor of what we
may call modernity. But the fact that the issue
itself can be so clearly documented in his work
and in that of other later natural philosophers, is
already a major contribution in its own right.

Aquinas: Thomas Aquinas was assuredly one
of the most perceptive contributors to discussions
of the nature of science in this period. His inter-
ests in the issue were, of course, primarily theo-

logical and not physical. Unlike his mentor, Albertus Magnus, he devoted little of his abundant energies to empirical inquiries into the natural world. Nonetheless, he was well-versed in the natural science of his day, particularly in astronomy.[45] His own most considerable "natural" work was his commentary on the *Physics* of Aristotle. The *Physics*, it should be remembered, is for the most part devoted to careful conceptual analysis. It begins from the ways in which certain very general terms are used in common speech and it systematically analyzes the consequences of these *legomena*.[46] It ranks itself, therefore, G. E. L. Owen remarks, "not with physics in our sense of the word, but with philosophy. Its data are for the most part the materials not of natural history but of dialectic, and its problems are accordingly not questions of empirical fact but conceptual puzzles".[47] In terms of the kind of evidence it relies on, it belongs rather more to the tradition of Parmenides than to that of the "physicists", as Aristotle calls them, despite its frequent references to the latter. *Physics* I, for example, seeks the necessary and sufficient conditions for the correct application of the term, 'change', and rests, not on a series of observations of different sorts of natural change, but upon the simple ability to use the term, 'change', correctly, an ability dependent on experience, of course, but only in the most general way.

Analysis of this kind falls naturally into a deductive pattern once the dialectical preparations are made. Aristotle sets out to *prove* his claims: that an actual infinite cannot exist, that motion cannot have had a beginning, and so on. But there are no demonstrations in the strict sense, since he is not dealing here with essences or natural kinds. The problems we have seen regarding twinkling stars and horned animals do not arise in "philosophy of nature", as this genre later came to be called. (An analogue of these problems may appear when causes are postulated, as for example in the case of continuing "violent" motion.) The most general terms in which we articulate our descriptions of the world around us ('motion', 'place', 'time') are assumed to refer in a straightforward way, and are given precising definitions, if necessary. No need, then, to test hypothesis against specific observations, or the like. As long as one stays with "philosophy of nature" in this sense, the problems we have been discussing in regard to demonstration in natural science do not appear. But they are apt to emerge, in different guises elsewhere, as indeed they do for Aquinas.

There is a tension in his thinking, it has often been suggested, in regard to our knowledge of sensible things.[48] On the one hand, he is emphatic in claiming that knowledge of the quiddities of natural things constitutes the appropriate object of the intellect: "The proper object of the human intellect is the quiddity of a material thing, [when that thing has been] apprehended by the senses and the imagination."[49] On the other hand, he also maintains that the essences of physical things are hidden from us: "Our power of knowing (*cognitio*) is so weak that no philosopher can ever fully discover the nature of a single fly."[50] "The essences of things are not known to us. . . ."[51] Commenting on the text of Aquinas, Jacques Maritain expresses the contrast in dramatic fashion: Is it not scandalous that though our intelligence has as its connatural object

> the essences of corporeal things, in face of them it meets such serious impediments that it has to be content, in a vast sector of our knowledge of nature, with the imperfect intellection we call "perinoetic"?[52]

The notion of an imperfect ("perinoetic") understanding is prompted by texts like these: "In sensible things, the essential differences are unknown to us, so they are signified by accidental differences which originate from the essential ones, as a cause is signified by its effect."[53] "Substantial forms are of themselves unknown to us; we learn about them from their proper accidents."[54] "Since we do not know essential differences, sometimes. . . we use accidents or effects in their place, and name a thing accordingly."[55] "Since substantial differences are unknown to us, or at least unnamed by us, it is sometimes necessary to use accidental differences in their place. . . for proper accidents are the effects of substantial forms and make them known to us."[56]

Aquinas was obviously far less optimistic than was Aristotle about the ability of the human intellect to extract a knowledge of essence from the regularities noted in perception. He recognizes that the features of sensible bodies that are accessible to human powers of perception are not, in general, part of essence; the forms abstracted by the mind in consequence of such perception are not substantial forms. We may *say* that fire is a simple, hot and dry body, but this is not to specify essence directly; rather it is to designate in terms of phenomenal qualities which are the effect of essence.[57] Can one infer from these effects back to their cause, essence? How *do* the proper accidents make the substantial forms known? Which of the two strands in his thinking are we to emphasize here, the pessimistic one (the essences of natural things are hidden from us) or the more optimistic strand (we can discover essences through the clues afforded by the proper accidents)? Or ought we combine these two:

essences of physical things are indeed initially hidden (i.e., we do not have *immediate* access to them in the intellectual processes involved in perception) but they can be progressively discovered by means of indirect modes of inference?

In support of this last suggestion:

> The human intellect must of necessity understand by composition and division. For since the intellect passes from potentiality to act, it has a likeness to generable things, which do not attain to perfection all at once but acquire it by degrees. In the same way, the human intellect does not acquire perfect knowledge of a thing by the first apprehension; but it first apprehends something of the thing, such as its quiddity, which is the first and proper object of the intellect; and then it understands the properties, accidents, and various dispositions affecting the essence. Thus it necessarily relates one thing with another by composition and division; and from one composition and division it necessarily proceeds to another, and this is *reasoning.*[58]

But how exactly does this reasoning work? "Composition" is a linking of attributes, "division" a separating. How is one to discover the *necessary* linkage he mentions? Are we back to postulating an ability of mind simply to *see* the necessity of a causal linkage once the attributes themselves are fully understood, the kind of ability that Aristotle had ultimately to invoke in *epagoge*? Aquinas gives us very little to go on here, and one reason is not far to seek. There were few, if any, plausible candidates for inference from accidents to essence in the natural science of his day. (Discussions of the nature of the rainbow might have afforded the best clue.) In one text, he suggests that the senses must be the arbiter in such a process:

> Sometimes the properties and accidents of a thing revealed by the sense adequately manifest its nature, and then the intellect's judgement of the thing's nature must conform to what the sense reveals about it. All natural things, limited to sensible matter, are of this sort. So the terminus of knowledge in natural science must be in the sense, so that we judge of natural things as the sense reveals them, as is clear in the *De Caelo*.[59]

What are the consequences of this initiative for the doctrine of demonstration? In his *Commentary on the Posterior Analytics*, Aquinas makes much of the distinction between demonstration *propter quid* and demonstration *quia*, to which only a single passage in the *Posterior Analytics* itself was devoted. A major reason for this shift in emphasis was undoubtedly the importance of the distinction for Aquinas' theology: we can arrive at demonstrative knowledge of God's existence, he argues, but the demonstration can never be better than *quia* since we lack the knowledge of essence, the appropriate definition, that a demonstration *propter quid* would require as middle term:

> From every effect the existence of its proper cause can be demonstrated [by a demonstration *quia*] so long as its effects are better known to us. . . . Hence the existence of God, since it is not self-evident to us, can be demonstrated from those of His effects which are known to us. . . . When the existence of a cause is demonstrated from an effect, this effect takes the place of the definition of the cause in proving the cause's existence. This is especially the case in regard to God, because in order to prove the existence of anything, it is necessary to accept as a middle term the meaning of the name, and not its essence, for the question of its essence follows on the question of its existence.[60]

The problem here, of course, as with any demonstration *quia*, would be (as we have seen) to prove convertibility, that is, to show that God is the only *possible* explanation of the effects in question, and to show this assertion itself to be *necessary*, to be something more than plausible hypothesis.

Aside from the elaboration of the *quia-propter quid* distinction, however, the discussion of demonstration in Aquinas' **Commentary** stays remarkably close to the original. The examples of the non-twinkling planets and the phases of the moon are presented without comment. First principles are said to be arrived at by means of induction, understood as an abstraction of universals from sensible particulars, many times experienced.[61] There is no hint as to how *exactly* the assertion of causal relationship is to be arrived at. If we have to infer from perceived phenomenal qualities back to the unperceived essence that is their cause, how is the universal corresponding to this essence to be formed? *Epagoge* may work to relate perceivable accidents, but how does it link those in turn with the substantial forms Aquinas holds to be causally responsible for them?[62] If the essences of sensible things are hidden, as Aquinas says they are, is not the role of *strict* demonstration in natural science so circumscribed as to be almost non-existent?

It is puzzling, on the face of it, that someone who had so clearly realized the seriousness of the barriers facing inquiry into natural essence would not have allowed some hint of this challenge to appear in his exposition of the canonical doctrine of demonstration in the *Posterior Analytics*. In a recent Aquinas Lecture, Alasdair MacIntyre argued that demonstration for Aristotle and Aquinas, as an "achieved and perfected knowledge", is an ideal constituting the *goal* of inquiry, one rarely perhaps reached.[63] Rational justification can thus take two quite different forms:

> Within the demonstrations of a perfected science, afforded by finally adequate formulations of first principles, justification proceeds by way of showing of any judgement either that it itself states such a first principle or that it is deducible from [one]. . . . But when we are engaged in an inquiry which has not yet achieved this perfected end state, that is, in the activities of almost every, perhaps every, science with which we are in fact acquainted, rational justification is of another kind.[64]

This second kind belongs first and foremost to dialectics. Principles will be formulated provisionally; "apodictic theses" will be tested against "empirical phenomena", and reformulated, if necessary, in the light of such tests.[65] Even the very *telos* of the inquiry itself, the conception of the sort of science that ought be aimed for, is open to modification in the light of results achieved along the way. Progress will thus "often be tortuous, uneven, move inquiry in more than one direction, and result in periods of regress and frustration. The outcome may even be large-scale defeat. . . ."[66] "What had been taken to be a set of necessary apodictic judgements, functioning as first principles, may always turn out to be false." Hence:

> No one could ever finally know whether the *telos/finis* of some particular natural science had been achieved or not. For it might well appear that all the conditions for the achievement of a finally-perfected science concerning some particular subject-matter had indeed been satisfied, and yet the fact that further investigation may always lead to the revision or rejection of what had previously been taken to be adequate formulations of first principles suggests that we could never be fully entitled to make this assertion.[67]

Such principles are "necessary", then, only in the weak sense that they are *stages* on the way to a true, but quite possibly unreachable, judgement that "presents to us actually how things are and cannot but be".[68]

What are we to make of this account? It affords a perceptive description of what might fairly be said to be the "received view" in contemporary philosophy of science of the status of theory in natural science. But can it claim a warrant in the text of the *Posterior Analytics* or of Aquinas' commentary on that work? MacIntyre allows that the Aristotelian-Thomistic tradition has to be supplemented here by the insights of such contemporaries as C. S. Peirce and Karl Popper in order to arrive at this highly fallibilist conception of science, one which construes "first principles" as tentative hypotheses open to continuing modification in the light of new observational evidence. But surely this is rather radical "supplementation"? What entitles us to call the resultant view "Aristotelian-Thomistic"? The transformation that has come about in the conception of natural science in modern times has been largely due to developments in empirical inquiry itself, to an internal dynamic working within the history of science; it is to be judged in the first place, then, by reference to the history of science. MacIntyre remarks that it is in the spirit of the Aristotelian-Thomist tradition to test a conception of inquiry against the actual history of that form of inquiry. This may be so, but the conception of inquiry that emerges from this testing may well diverge from the Aristotelian tradition sufficiently to make the claim that it is a natural extension of the doctrine of the *Posterior Analytics* a rather forced one.

There are two sticking points in the way of such a continuity thesis. The warrant for an Aristotelian demonstration lies ultimately in the recognition on the part of the intellect that the premisses, properly understood, are "self-evident", i.e., carry their own internal warrant. MacIntyre himself seems to say as much. Argument *to* first principles, he notes:

> cannot be a matter of dialectic and nothing more, since the strongest conclusions of dialectic remain a matter only of belief, not of knowledge. What more is involved? The answer is an act of the understanding which begins from but goes beyond what dialectic and induction provide, in formulating a judgement as to what is necessarily the case in respect of whatever is informed by some essence. . . . Insight, not inference, is involved here. . . .[69]

This catches the rationalist aspect of *epagoge*, to be sure. But then he imposes a significant qualification: the judgement of the intellect in regard to essence still has to contend with "constraints" imposed by dialectical and inductive considerations, and the insight it affords requires "further vindication", namely, a check as to whether the proposed premisses/principles *do*, in fact, provide a "causal explanation of the known empirical facts".

Insight into "what is necessarily the case" is, therefore, apparently not of itself sufficient to warrant the first principle, the premiss of the demonstration. Quite complex-sounding forms of inference, continuing tests of the proposed principle against the empirical facts, are also needed. It is difficult, however, to find a justification for this restriction in the text of the *Posterior Analytics* itself. The claims made there for the *nous* that is consequent upon *epagoge* show no such hesitation, as we have seen. But perhaps it is to the text of Aquinas (though not, it would seem, to his commentary on the *Posterior Analytics*) that we ought to be looking. One relevant passage:

> The ultimate end which the investigation of reason ought to reach is the understanding of principles, in which we resolve our judgements. And when this takes place, it is not called a rational procedure or proof but a demonstration. Sometimes, however, the investigation of reason cannot arrive at the ultimate end, but stops in the investigation itself, that is when two possible solutions

still remain open to the investigator. And this happens when we proceed by means of probable arguments, which are suited to produce opinion or belief, but not science. In this sense, rational method is contradistinguished to demonstrative method, and we can proceed rationally in all the sciences in this way, preparing the way for necessary proofs by probable arguments.[70]

This is much more promising. But it raises new questions. These "probable arguments" can produce only "opinion". How does the transition to a first principle actually come about, then? How do the probable arguments prepare the way for demonstration proper? Does a demonstration arrived at in this way *rest* in any respect on the probable arguments? It would seem not, for if it did, it would remain provisional. And its warrant would no longer be self-evidence. But if it does not rest on them, why were they needed? There is an unresolved difficulty here, one that will surface again much later in Descartes' *Discourse on Method*. The divide between science and opinion, legacy of Greek ways of thinking, represents a sharp dichotomy, not a continuum. MacIntyre suggests, as we have seen, that demonstrative science is to be regarded as an ideal that lies at the horizon of inquiry. This has the merit of deflecting the troublesome problem of how the transition can ever be made from opinion to science: in practice, it is *never* made or at least we can never *know* that it has been. What the scientists of today would call "science" would, therefore, have to be labelled "opinion", or at least something other than science. And the traditional Aristotelian claim that the human intellect can, on the basis of sense-experience, directly grasp the relation between a particular kind of effect and its proper cause in a definitive way, would have to be either set aside or at the very least forcefully reinterpreted.

There is a further sticking-point in the way of those who seek to establish a strong continuity between the Aristotelian and the contemporary conceptions of science. The phenomenalist cast of Aristotle's account of *epagoge* has already been noted. It imposes a severe restriction on the concepts available for deployment in a demonstration. To demonstrate in natural science is to discover a causal relationship between *perceptible* features of sensible bodies, features that are regularly found together. Aquinas comments:

> If universals, from which demonstration proceeds, could be grasped apart from induction, it would follow that someone could acquire *scientia* of things which he could not sense. But it is impossible for universals to be grasped apart from induction.[71]

Universals can come to be known *only* through induction (*epagoge*). Or in the idiom of abstraction, the concepts in terms of which a science of sensible bodies is to be constructed can only originate in perception: the form can come to exist in the mind only if it be abstracted from sensible instances of that form. An oft-quoted scholastic maxim made this restriction quite explicit: *nihil est in intellectu quod non prius fuerit in sensu.*

But now let us return one further time to the non-twinkling planets. As we have seen, Aristotle himself attempted a theoretical explanation of the proposed causal link between distance and twinkling in terms of the attenuation of visual rays emitted from the eye of the observer. These visual rays are clearly not themselves observable, nor is their attenuation. And their attenuation may itself require the introduction of further theoretical entities to explain it. Explanations of this sort are dotted throughout Aristotle's work, particularly the **Meteorology**. The all-important spheres on which the circular motions of the celestial bodies are said to depend would furnish the most striking example.

When Aristotle is faced with the need to show that the link between two kinds of feature is a genuinely causal one, he quite often in practice postulates an underlying structure or process not itself observable, instead of just relying on the assertion that the link can be intuitively *seen* to be a necessary one. The necessity is thus mediated by the postulated entity; the causal link is held to be necessary in *virtue* of this entity. But where is the requisite universal to come from? There are universals for A and B (twinkling and distance) but not, it would seem, for C (the visual ray). C has to be somehow constructed in imagination, relying on elements drawn from perception in other contexts, no doubt. But the *nature* of C is constructed mentally in response to the request for explanation; it is not the result of abstraction. The test of this constructed concept lies in its ability to *explain*, not in its being properly abstracted from sensible particulars. The shift from abstraction to construction means that the resultant form of inference cannot be demonstration, unless the requirements for demonstration be greatly weakened, not to say transformed.

Neither Aristotle nor Aquinas addresses this problem. Aquinas' detailed account of the abstraction characteristic of natural science (the first degree of abstraction from matter) gives no hint that something other than straightforward abstraction may be needed at the crucial moment in constructing causal explanations.[72] Nevertheless, if one looks at what he has to say, not about natural science, but about "divine science", a possible response suggests itself. We *can* come to know things that transcend sense and abstraction-based imagination, he says, by beginning from the level of sense and imagination and then arguing from this level as from an effect to a cause which surpasses it.[73] We cannot be said to know the nature of such a cause (answering to *quid est*?), only that it exists (answering to *an est*?). Still, in order to know that a thing is, *something* must be known of what it is. Thus, in order to know that God and other immaterial beings exist, we have to be able to postulate something, at least, of what they are or, at least, of what they are not.[74] When the cause so transcends the effect as God does the physical universe, "we take the effect only as the starting-point to prove the existence of the cause and some of its conditions [e.g., the power to create], although the quiddity of the cause is always unknown".[75]

The barrier here to knowability is difference of nature, and ultimately transcendence of nature. And the response is to construct an incomplete and imperfect definition of a cause that would be sufficient and (more problematically) necessary to account for significant general features of the world of sense. This is, in striking ways, similar to the sort of construction that a retroduction from effect to cause in natural science might also require. The visual ray does not transcend the sensible order as God does, but it does differ enough from it in regard to its accessibility to human modes of perception that a not-entirely-dissimilar constructive form of inference has to be employed to reach it. One could say, then, that the sort of retroduction that Aquinas employs to enable him to affirm the existence of God and the angels *might* have suggested how to proceed in natural science when causes inaccessible to sense appear to be required. Admittedly, Aquinas specifically excludes this parallel, insisting that natural science and divine science differ precisely on this point.[76] Nevertheless, a way out has been, if not opened, then at least indicated, and the tight requirements of demonstration *propter quid* have been found incapable of satisfaction in least one domain of science, and a weaker alternative has been allowed.

It would be wrong, of course, to suggest that this relaxation is what actually led to the later acceptance of theoretical and non-demonstrative forms of inference in natural science. The change took a very long time, and the main inspiration for the change came from progress in the natural sciences themselves. It gradually came to be realized that the causal agencies underlying explanation in the natural sciences, if not as remote from abstractive terms anchored in perception as Aquinas had declared God to be, still required a

new and non-abstractive approach to the concepts
required to define them.

   Galileo and the Paduan tradition: One other
philosopher should be mentioned in that context,
Jacopo Zabarella, with whom yet another continuity thesis has been linked. There is space here only
to summarize the argument; doing it justice would
require a full-length study. J. H. Randall suggested in a wide-ranging work, *The School of
Padua and the Emergence of Modern Science*
(1961), that Galileo's notions of scientific method
were heavily dependent on the traditions of the
school where he spent much of his teaching
career, Padua, and particularly on the logical
works of Zabarella:

   The logic and methodology taken over and
   expressed by Galileo and destined to
   become the scientific method of the seventeenth century physicists. . . was even more
   clearly the result of a fruitful critical recon-
   struction of the Aristotelian theory of science, undertaken at Padua in particular. . . .
   [In] its completed statement in the logical
   controversies of Zabarella. . . it reaches the
   form familiar in Galileo. . . .[77]

The claim gave rise to a lively controversy. Two objections, in particular, were raised. One was that the connections between Galileo and Zabarella had not been clearly enough established, that although there were some resonances between the logical terms used by Galileo here and there in his scientific works, there was no real evidence of influence and no obvious medium for it. The second objection was that Randall had conflated logic and methodology. It was one thing to say that Galileo's logic (more exactly, his conception of science, his view of what kind of knowledge-claim *scienza* makes) had some affinities with that of the Paduan tradition. But it was quite another to claim that his *methodology*, the methodology that laid such a distinctive stamp on the natural science of those who followed him, also derived from Padua. This seemed far less plausible; indeed, it found (and would still find) few defenders. Galileo gradually evolved a complex methodology involving controlled experiment, repeated measurement, mathematical idealization, and much more, which was strongly opposed by his Paduan Aristotelian colleagues and certainly finds few resonances in their tradition. Since it was his methodology and, of course, his actual discoveries in mechanics and elsewhere, and not merely his concept of science, that shaped what came after, the Randall thesis was generally thought to fail, or at least to be greatly overstated.

In the last ten years, it has been restated and strengthened by William Wallace. Zabarella still retains his role, but the thesis has been broadened. The "canons" of Galileo's new science, and hence of science in the Galilean tradition, Wallace suggests, "were those of Aristotle's *Posterior Analytics* read with the eyes of Aquinas, and appropriated by him from the Jesuits of the Collegio Romano".[78] Wallace has shown, to most people's satisfaction, that two short commentaries on logical topics, dismissed by the editor of the National Edition of Galileo's works as juvenile school-pieces, were written by Galileo in his mid-twenties when he was just beginning his career as a teacher of mathematics and natural philosophy.[79] Further, by a remarkably painstaking piece of detective work, Wallace has also shown that these two pieces are almost entirely derivative from lecture-notes composed by some contemporary Jesuit teachers of natural philosophy at the Collegio Romano, notably the notes of a certain Paolo Valla. And Valla drew heavily on Zabarella as well as on the Thomist tradition. What this establishes is that Galileo was cognizant of the Jesuit, and indirectly of the Paduan, tradition of commentary on the *Posterior Analytics*, notably on the topic of demonstration, to which one of the

two sets of his notes is devoted. Whether (as
Wallace supposes) the notes represented Galileo's
own views, then or later, is a quite different matter. That Galileo should have carefully summa-
rized and paraphrased portions of the lecture
notes of senior colleagues, who were teaching the
courses he himself might be called on to teach,
does not give strong reason to describe these
notes as conveying his *own* "logical doctrine".

Several features of this doctrine are said to
mark the scientific work of Galileo's maturity. On
this the continuity claim rests. First and foremost
is the alleged appearance of the *regressus* form of
argument characteristic of the Paduan Aristotelian tradition, and especially of Zabarella's logic.
The *regressus* was the combination of the *quia* and
propter quid inferences we have already seen, the
first establishing the existence and something of
the nature of the purported cause and the second
demonstrating the effect from this cause.
Zabarella and his colleagues had developed an
elaborate analysis of this back-and-forward mode
of explanation. (Jardine describes Zabarella's theory as one of "vast and obsessive complexity".[80])
Crucial to this analysis was the occurrence of a
period of consideration or reflection (*negotiatio* or
investigatio) between the back-to-cause and
forward-to-effect phases. The first of these phases
yields an indistinct (*confusa*) notion of the cause.

The intellect then wrestles with this notion, some-how clarifies it, and finally comprehends the cause sufficiently to allow the *propter quid* demonstra-tion to be completed with assurance. In particular, the intellect is said to have the ability to "see" that the crucial convertibility condition holds (equivalently ruling out the possibility of alter-native causes).

Though this intermediate phase cannot sim-ply reduce to the *epagoge* of the **Posterior Analytics** (which is required before the first phase can even get under way), the attribution to the intellect of the ability to discern the nature of the required cause is reminiscent of the traditional doctrine of *nous*. There can be no doubt that the intention of the Paduan Aristotelians was to show how the *regressus* could provide *strictly* demonstrative explanations. It would be tempting to take the intermediate phase as a forerunner of later hypo-thetical modes of explanation, but Wallace and Jardine are surely correct in excluding this read-ing.[81] Hence, if Galileo is to be seen as a propo-nent of the *regressus* notion of proof, he has also to be construed as a defender of Aristotelian demonstration as the appropriate mode of proof in natural science.

Jardine, to the contrary, argues that far from promoting *regressus*, Galileo was actively critical of its use as a model of proof:

> Galileo was well aware of the contemporary
> Aristotelian theory of scientific demonstra-
> tion, had a sure insight into its weaknesses,
> rejected it outright, and set up in its place
> as a crucial part of his propaganda for the
> union of mathematics and natural philoso-
> phy a method of inquiry modelled on a
> classical account of the quest for proofs in
> geometry.[82]

The first thing to say here is that in the works
of his scientific maturity Galileo never alludes to
the method of *regressus* one way or the other,
either to affirm it or reject it. True, he frequently
uses the term 'demonstration', but it carries with
it the connotation of 'convincing proof', no more.
And he links it quite often with mathematics;
phrases like 'the rigor of geometrical demonstration', 'the purest mathematical demonstration'
support Jardine's argument that Galileo's notion
of demonstration is associated by him much more
explicitly with geometry than with the syllogism.[83]
To the extent that the properties of necessity and
of convertibility appear, it is because of the mathematical form in which his arguments in mechanics are conveyed. Since he sets aside causal
explanation in terms of gravity, and confines himself to kinematical measures of space and time
only, the issue central to *regressus* (arguing from
effect to efficient cause) simply does not arise in

his mechanics. Furthermore, he returns again and again to the Platonic-Archimedean theme of "impediments", the various obstacles that arise when one tries to apply an idealized mathematical system to the complexity of the material world.[84] Such a system applies only approximately, and approximation is something that has no place in the classic conception of demonstration *propter quid*. A necessary truth about nature cannot be just *approximately* true.

Galileo's law of falling bodies affords a clear illustration. It is the *Aristotelian* in the dialogues, Simplicio, who keeps objecting that the necessity one finds in purely mathematical inference cannot readily be transferred to claims about the material world. As long as Galileo's account of uniformly accelerated motion be taken simply as a mathematical definition, the issue of demonstration does not arise. It is the claim that this is, *in fact*, the sort of motion that occurs were a body to fall *in vacuo* at the earth's surface that raises the problem. Galileo gives two sorts of arguments in support of his claim. One is that uniform acceleration is the simplest mathematical form that this motion could take and hence is the one that Nature would employ. The other is that the assumption that *in vacuo* fall is, in fact, uniformly accelerated is supported by the "very powerful reason" that it "corresponds to that which physical experiments show to the senses".[85] The first is reminiscent of strict demonstration: Galileo is asking us to see that motion *must* take place in this way. (But, of course, we know from Newton's vantage-point that the law is *not* exact. The acceleration of *in vacuo* fall gradually increases. Nature does *not* always act in the simplest way.) Galileo relies also on a second line of argument, which is that consequences drawn from the assumption of uniformly accelerated motion can be experimentally verified. But, of course, this is no longer a demonstrative form of argument: it rests on the extent to which, and the precision with which, the consequences of the supposition have been observationally verified. There is no suggestion that falling motion must *necessarily* follow this law.

Wallace responds to this objection:

Galileo's way of presenting and justifying this definition [of the motion of fall *in vacuo*] has elicited criticism from some, who see him as employing a hypothetico-deductive method such as characterizes modern scientific investigations, and thus as falling into the fallacy of *affirmatio consequentis* when using the implied consequences of his definition to support it as the antecedent. It is true that the definition can be regarded as a *suppositio*, and therefore that the demonstrations to follow are made *ex suppositione.* . . . From a formal point of view, moreover, a *suppositio* has the character of an *ipotesi* [hypothesis], and thus its value might be judged by its ability to save the appearances, regardless of whether or not it describes a situation that is actually verified in the order of nature. It is for this reason that Galileo repeatedly makes the distinction between *supposizioni* that are true and absolute in nature, and those that are false and made purely for the sake of computation. . . . Galileo's principles, the definition of naturally accelerated motion included, must stand or fall on their own merits, and not merely on the basis of one or two consequences drawn from them.[86]

This long quotation is instructive. It helps us understand why Wallace is so averse to allowing Galileo's science to be called hypothetico-deductive and why he labors so hard to drape it in the mantle of the Aristotelian-Thomist tradition. Unless Galilean mechanics can be construed as demonstrative, it is reduced to simply "saving the appearances", thus separating it from what "is actually verified in the order of nature". There are echoes here of the distrust among Aristotelian natural philosophers of the late Middle Ages for the epicycles of the Ptolemaic astronomers, and the philosophers' way of dismissing as "fictive" (the alternative to "demonstrative" that Wallace often employs) anything which simply rests on "saving the appearances". But Galileo's constant appeal to "the very powerful reason" that one of his suppositions is verified by the consequences drawn from it *is* appealing to the "appearances", i.e., the experimental results. Those who see Galileo as employing hypothetical forms of inference on occasion do *not* (as Wallace suggests) take this to imply that this makes his reasoning fallacious. They would reject the over-simple dichotomy between demonstrative and fictive, and maintain that a hypothetical argument, one supported by the consequences drawn from it, can have any degree of likelihood up to practical (not, however, absolute) certainty. Insofar as Galileo's argument for his law of fall *did* carry force, it was because of the fact that it *did* so successfully "save the appearances", i.e., fit the phenomena of experiment. If there was fallacy, it might be said that it was in Galileo's appeal to the simplicity of Nature, in his vain attempt to present the appearance of strict demonstration.

Galileo's telescopic discoveries opened up for discussion a host of questions about the natures of the beings now coming into view: sunspots, comets, and the like. There were surprises too in regard to the lunar surface, the variable illumination of Venus, and four small points of light that seemed to accompany Jupiter. Galileo's method in dealing with these phenomena was to postulate a cause which might explain the observed phenomena, and try to find as much evidence as possible in support of his hypothesis. There was nothing particularly mysterious about this method; it is, when all is said and done, little more than common sense. Would it have been inhibited or favored by an appeal to the *regressus* tradition? One could, perhaps, argue either way. But the negative side is surely the stronger. The *regressus* tradition *did* insist on convertibility, on finding a cause to which one could infer with *necessity* from the effect to be explained, and on an interval of intellectual reflection on the nature of the proposed cause. The Paduans had assuredly never taken *negotiatio* to designate a period when alternatives are systematically explored, anomalies dissolved, and further positive evidence accumulated.

In some favorable cases, like the inference that mountains are the cause of certain variable shadows on the lunar surface, Galileo could infer *almost* directly from effect to cause, that is, exclude alternative possible explanations with a high degree of assurance. This does not, however, make his proof demonstrative in the Aristotelian sense. What made his supposition amount to certainty in his own mind was that it accounted so neatly for the appearances. But it could not be *deduced* from them; several (highly plausible) assumptions had to be made which in turn would require support from the consequences drawn from them. Commenting, Wallace allows that such assumptions are in fact present and remarks that until Galileo could be assured of the truth of such auxiliary assumptions, all he had was "opinion" and not "science". (Once again, this is too sharp a dichotomy; instead, there is a spectrum of likelihood ascending as far as practical certainty.[87]) Wallace goes on to note that Galileo was aware of an objection to his claim about mountains on the moon. If there are lunar mountains, how can the edge of the lunar disk be seen as quite smooth in the telescope? He attempted to dissolve the objection, but it was not until 1664 that telescopes were sufficiently powerful to show that the moon's outline *is* in fact slightly irregular. Does this mean that until 1664, all that astronomers had was *opinion* in regard to the lunar mountains? And that it became science with the 1664 observation? And, in any event, does not the dependence of the case for lunar mountains on this observational consequence show how artificial it is to force Galileo's argument into the mold of Aristotelian demonstration, one purporting to yield "certain knowledge based on true causes"?[88]

Nothing has been said about Galileo's use of the phrase '*ex suppositione*', another supposed link to earlier logical doctrines and specifically to the Thomist tradition of commentary on the *Posterior Analytics*.[89] Nor has an adequate distinction been drawn between what Galileo *believed* himself to be doing and what, from our perspective, he was *actually* doing. When tracing his links with earlier logical traditions, it is the former that is the more important; in assessing his influence on his successors in regard to this issue, it might be the latter that one would stress. Galileo was quick, often too quick in our estimate, to claim certainty for his conclusions. And in mechanics, at least, he sought principles which would, as far as possible, carry conviction in their own right. On the issue that meant most to him, that of the double motion of the earth, he sought for proof in such supposed consequences as the ebb and flow of tides, and the curved paths of the sunspots. The more acute kinematical arguments for the earth's motions, showing how much more "natural" it is to attribute motion to the earth than to attach various sorts of motions to the heavenly bodies, he called "plausible reasons", and remarked: "I do not pretend to draw a necessary proof from them, merely a greater probability".[90]

In short, Galileo aimed when he could at demonstration, in the sense of conclusive proof. But when this was not available, he would settle for as high a degree of probability as the evidence would warrant, showing no inclination to regard the resultant merely as "opinion". He used consequential modes of argument all the time, but never formulated a "method of hypothesis" and would probably have been reluctant to regard such a method as "the" method of science. All in all, then, even though Galileo was fond of using the term 'demonstration', there is little to warrant the claim that he was influenced in a significant way by the elaborations of the notion of demonstration in the older tradition of the *Posterior Analytics*.

As one looks at later seventeenth-century natural science, one immediately notices a significant difference between mechanics and the other sciences. In the mechanics of Descartes as of Newton, there was an emphasis on demonstration, on certainty, a suspicion of hypothesis. Perhaps this might be seen as an echo of the Aristotelian requirements for *episteme*, though in a mathematicized context remote from that of the *Posterior Analytics*. On the other hand, in other parts of natural philosophy, in optics, in chemistry, there was a growing realization that hypothesis is not only unavoidable, but even respectable, and efforts were made to formulate criteria in terms of

which it should be judged. Both of these strands
are already found in different parts of Galileo's
work; there is thus no *single* "Galilean" heritage
in that regard."[1]

Part Three: Inductivism

In deference to the occasion, we have spent
so long on assaying the stability of some of the
bridges that recent scholars have thrown across
the gap between the tradition of the *Posterior
Analytics* and modern views on what constitutes
the basic form of scientific inference that we are
going to have to telescope these later views in a
rather summary way. The earlier emphasis on
demonstration was not entirely lost; indeed, it
took daring form in Kant's *Metaphysical Foundations of Natural Science*. But two other kinds of
inference more or less supplanted demonstration
as the paradigm of the scientist. (Demonstration
remained a will-o'-the-wisp for those who took
mechanics as the paradigm of science; it is all too
easy to see its conceptual structure, whether in its
Newtonian or more recent relativistic forms, as so
luminous as also to be necessary.) One of these
types of inference has a familiar label: 'induction'.
The other (which we shall call "retroduction")
even still has not, which is rather extraordinary.

Nominalism: "Modernity" began, as everyone knows, with the *via moderna* of the fourteenth century, which was "modern" in part because of its rejection of the notion of demonstration central to the Aristotelian tradition it opposed. The notion of necessity that the possibility of demonstration in natural science conveyed seemed to a great many theologians, from the first introduction of the Aristotelian "natural" works in the early thirteenth century onwards, to require an unacceptable restriction on God's freedom in creating, and an equally unacceptable determinism of causal action on the part of creatures. The fourth of the 219 propositions condemned by Bishop Tempier in 1277 rejects the claim "that one should not hold anything unless it is self-evident or can be manifested from self-evident principles".[92] The idea that the human mind can, on the grounds of reflection, on what is perceived, affirm a necessary relation between cause and effect was regarded as a challenge to the notion of miracle so central to the Christian economy.

The nominalism of Ockham, and especially the more extreme versions of that nominalism in the works of Nicholas d'Autrecourt, Jean de Mirecourt and Robert Holkot, presented an alternative to the Aristotelian scheme in which the emphasis has shifted from the universal to the particular, from demonstration to induction.

Induction itself in one sense resembles the *epagoge* of the earlier tradition because it begins from observed regularities of co-occurrence in the sensible world. But it differs in a crucial way: instead of the intellect's going on to grasp the nature of the cause sufficiently clearly to allow an unqualified affirmation of necessary connection between cause and particular effect to be made, induction according to Ockham rests simply on the evidence of the co-occurrences and has the degree (and only the degree) of logical force that this conveys. It is further dependent on a principle of uniformity of nature which itself has to be regarded as hypothetical, since it rests on the ordination of God's will to a common course of nature, which is not absolute but, in principle at least, open to exception. One thing is said to be the efficient cause of another if in the presence of the first the second follows, nothing more. A causal relation between A and B cannot, therefore, be known *a priori*; it can be learnt only from the repeated experience of their conjunction. Induction is thus a matter of *generalization* from a limited set of instances of a regularity. It is, if you will, a kind of sampling.

Nicholas goes on to draw a more skeptical conclusion than Ockham had done. Since the existence of effects cannot strictly entail the existence of corresponding causes, the best that one can aspire to in natural science is a degree of probability. The attempt to infer to essence or substance from perceived particulars must necessarily beg the question. In turning away so decisively from the ideal of demonstration, Nicholas is not especially advocating the importance in human terms of empirical investigation: what little can be learned (he says) can be learned in a short while, but it must be learned from *things*, not from the works of Aristotle.[93] There has been a great deal of discussion among historians of later medieval thought in late years about the influence of nominalist ideas on the origins of modern science. Our concern here is with the notion of induction only. The nominalists advocated the substitution of induction (in the sense of generalization) for demonstration as the paradigm mode of inference in natural science, challenging the fundamental notion of nature on which the earlier account had rested. But they did not work this up into a formal account of method in natural science.

Bacon: That was left to Francis Bacon, and this brings us to the second significant moment in the long story of inductivism. In the *New Organon* (1620), Bacon proposed a new method which was to replace that of the *Posterior Analytics*. He saw the two methods as diametrically opposed:

There can be only two ways of searching into and discovering truth. The one flies from the senses and particulars to the most general axioms, and from these principles, the truth of which it takes for settled and immovable, proceeds to judgement and to the discovery of middle axioms. And this way is now in fashion. The other derives axioms from the senses and particulars, rising by a gradual and unbroken ascent, so that it arrives at the most general axioms last of all. This is the true way, but as yet untried.[94]

Bacon tries to find a middle position between the essentialism of Aristotle and the more extreme forms of nominalism:

Though in nature nothing really exists besides individual bodies, performing pure individual acts according to a fixed law, yet in philosophy this very law, and the investigation, discovery, and explanation of it, is the foundation as well of knowledge as of operation. And it is this law with its clauses that I mean when I speak of *forms*, a name which I the rather adopt because it has grown into use and become familiar.[95]

There is a shift here from forms, understood as intrinsic to natural things, to forms understood as *laws*, as modes of action extrinsically imposed by a Lawgiver. These latter can still be called "eternal and immutable", and hence the natural philosopher can still aim at certainty. But the mode of attaining it is quite different.

Bacon sets out to construct natural histories organized by tables of presence, absence and degree (from which J. S. Mill much later got his methods of Sameness, Difference, and Concomitant Variation). These tables link regularly co-occurring factors; this is what for Bacon defines induction. The evidence *for* causal relationship comes from finding factors either invariably linked in observation or co-varying in a significant way. Evidence *against* is provided by absence, when presence might have been expected. The method is, thus, one of generalization, with an element of testing provided by the tables of absence.[96] Such a method "leaves but little to acuteness and strength of wits, but places all wits and understandings nearly on a level".[97] (There is some disagreement as to how seriously he meant this.) And it provides "not pretty and probable conjectures, but certain and demonstrable knowledge".[98] Again this would need to be qualified. For one thing, he stresses the "dullness, incompetency and deceptions of the senses".[99] For another, he treats his "axioms" as plausible conjectures meant to be tested by the "trial by fire" that crucial experiment can afford. Still, he does assume that at the end of that sometimes laborious process, a causal link that is "sure and indissoluble" can be found.[100]

Though Bacon is trying very hard to separate himself from the Aristotelian tradition, one can still catch echoes of *epagoge* here. In particular, he is seeking to discover regular and reliable correlations; his "laws", though their ontological basis is quite different, loosely correspond to the "natures" of the older tradition. The process of discovery, an "act of the intellect" left unexplained by Aristotle, is not spelled out in terms of the logical procedures to be followed. Bacon provides, then, not just a conception of what counts as science, but a general *methodology* to enable that goal to be attained.

If this were all, then Bacon could be presented as the inductivist *par excellence*, his aphorisms constituting the "Ur" text for those concerned to lay out the method of induction. But as we shall see in more detail later, a second quite different sort of inference is also hinted at in the pages of the **New Organon**. It is doubtful that Bacon was aware of the tension between the two methods or of the incompleteness of induction without the other mode of inference to back it up.

Induction is a matter of noting correlations between *observables*; unless *both* elements related by the "law" are observable, a correlation between them obviously cannot be discovered, on the basis of sense-evidence alone. Even if one were to extend the notion of *observation* (and Bacon was surprisingly wary of such an extension, recommending against a dependence on the new-fangled instruments just then coming into use), it would still be true that inductive method is strictly limited to factors that are observable in *some* sense. How, then, is the story to be extended to unobservables? Bacon in his famous discussion of the nature of heat in Book II of the *New Organon* showed himself perfectly willing to assert that the "heat" of a body is to be understood in terms of the motions of imperceptibly small parts of the body. We shall, however, leave this question aside for the moment in order to complete this quick survey of significant moments in the development of ideas about induction.

Hume: Hume's contribution was of a different sort, closer in spirit to that of Nicholas d'Autrecourt (whose name he had almost certainly never heard of) than of Bacon. Though in the introduction to the youthful *Treatise of Human Nature* (1739), he had promised "a complete system of the sciences, built on a foundation almost entirely new", in practice, he left the natural sci-

ences to Newton and his heirs, content to take
Newton at his word that the method of these sciences is inductive:

> And although the arguments from exper-
> iments and observations by induction be no
> demonstration of general conclusions, yet it
> is the best way of arguing which the nature
> of things admits of, and may be looked on
> as so much the stronger, by how much the
> induction is more general.[101]

Hume's interest was not specifically in
induction as it occurs in natural science. His challenge was to inductive procedure generally,
whether in the routines of daily life or in the more
technical pursuits of the natural philosopher.
"Reasoning concerning matters of fact" (he did
not use the term, 'induction') is, according to him,
founded on the relation of cause and effect, which
in turn reduces to a combination of constant conjunction, contiguity and temporal succession. The
idea of necessary connection, which we also associate with the causal relationship, can be explained as an expectation brought about by association or habit. But such an expectation in no way
justifies the prediction that C, which has been
constantly conjoined with E in the past, will once
again be followed by E on the next occasion. This
skeptical undermining of the rationality of belief

in the logical force of inductive inference offers no threat to daily living or to the natural sciences, according to Hume, but only because it is powerless to overcome the natural sentiments and convictions that govern daily life.

This is the famous "problem of induction" which went almost unnoticed among Hume's first readers but which has so intrigued twentieth-century analytic philosophers.[102] If one accepts Hume's starting-points, that all our ideas are derived from sense-impressions or inner feelings, and that causal relationship reduces to nothing more than the fact of constant conjunction in the past of certain classes of sense-impressions lacking any intrinsic connection, then indeed it *would* be difficult to warrant belief in induction. (One can never, of course, conclusively *prove* that on a given occasion E *must* follow C; Hume's use of the phrase 'demonstrative reasoning' is part of the problem here.) But then, of course, these same starting-points would not enable us to distinguish between genuine laws and accidental correlations. And causal inference to underlying structure is excluded. Hume's radical empiricism could take account neither of law nor of theory, as these had come to be understood in the natural science of the previous century.

If the only form of non-deductive inference *were* to be the inductive one, as empiricists have always tended to believe, then Hume's problem would still pose a troublesome challenge. It might perhaps be too easy to say that the famous "problem" is an artifact, that it vanishes if this faulty assumption be rejected. But, as we shall see, if the right form of non-deductive inference be recognized, genuine laws and accidental generalizations can be readily distinguished and the connection between cause and effect becomes something more than constant conjunction.

J. S. Mill: The fourth moment in the tale of induction can be kept a brief one. Mill's *System of Logic* (1843) may be called the "Inductivist Manifesto". There is only one type of non-deductive inference, and that is induction, understood as a straightforward procedure of generalization or sampling: "It consists in inferring from some individual instances in which a phenomenon is observed to occur, that it occurs in all instances of a certain class."[103] This method, properly used, enables the "ultimate laws of nature" to be discovered. Its validity rests upon a general principle of uniformity of nature. (His attempt to rest this principle in turn upon a broader induction is clearly fallacious.) Since causal relations hold only between observables, there can be no inference to unobservables. It need hardly be said that at the very time Mill was writing, the growing reliance of natural scientists on non-inductive inference to and from unobservables was leading to dramatic advances in fields like optics, chemistry, and theory of gases.

Logical Positivism: The best-remembered moment in the story occurred in our own century. A brief reminder of the salient points must suffice. The logical positivists used the term, 'induction', to cover all forms of non-deductive inference. Carnap attempted, unsuccessfully, to construct a theory of logical probability, what he called an "inductive logic", that would link hypothesis and evidence by means of some sort of "credence function". Such a logic, he believed, would provide the rules for inductive thinking, thus enabling rational choices to be made between hypotheses. He rejected the traditional view of inductive reasoning that would make it an inference from premises (evidence) to conclusion (usually a law), proposing instead that it is an assessment of the credibility of a particular hypothesis in the light of specific evidence, however the hypothesis be arrived at.[104] The hypothesis itself might be a law, a singular prediction, or a theory. And the logic, though a logic of induction (in Carnap's sense of the term), was deductive in form, enabling him (he hoped) to evade Hume's challenge.

Much more commonly, however, the focus of positivist concern was on how to get from the singular observation statements from which science begins to the laws of which they believed "finished" science to consist. Induction in this case would involve something like the traditional methods of Sameness, Difference, and Concomitant Variation, that Mill had taken over from the works of Bacon and John Herschel.[105] It would essentially be a special kind of sampling. The "laws" arrived at in this way would, thus, be empirical generalizations. But not all laws are of this sort. Besides empirical laws, there are also "theoretical" laws, those that make use of "theoretical" terms, i.e., terms that refer to hypothetical (unobservable) entities.[106] But how are *these* "laws" to be arrived at? Not by means of inductive generalization clearly. Carnap saw the difficulty:

How can theoretical laws be discovered? We cannot say: "Let's just collect more and more data, then generalize beyond the empirical laws until we reach theoretical ones." No theoretical law was ever found that way. . . . We never reach a point at which we observe a molecule. . . . For this reason, no amount of generalization from observations will ever produce a theory of molecular processes. Such a theory must

arise in another way. It is stated not as a
generalization of facts but as a hypothesis.
The hypothesis is then tested in a manner
analogous in certain ways to the testing of
an empirical law.[107]

"Analogous", perhaps, but exhibiting important differences. Carnap was struggling toward a
sharper distinction between theory and law, and
between the processes of inference involved in
each of these. But it was difficult to admit another
mode of inference. An empiricist could never feel
entirely easy with theoretical terms. And the "logical empiricists", as the group preferred to be
called in its later years, went to great lengths to
contrive devices like "correspondence rules" to
get around the hard fact that theoretical laws
could simply *not* be derived from empirical laws,
indeed that the term 'law' here is close to equivocal.[108] Their ambivalence towards a distinctively
theoretical mode of inference led, in turn, to a
famous ambivalence in regard to the existence of
theoretical entities. Their instinct as positivists
and empiricists was to regard theoretical terms
simply as heuristic devices. But a growing appreci-
ation of the difficulties to which this led would
eventually encourage some of them, at least, to
embrace a somewhat hesitant realism.[109]

So far, explanation has not been mentioned in this discussion of logical positivism. The well-known deductive-nomological (D-N) model proposed by Hempel and Paul Oppenheim took *laws* to be the primary explainers, and individual events to be the normal explananda. The apparent symmetry between explanation and prediction to which this led gave rise to problems severe enough to force the abandonment of the model. Explanation could simply not be reduced to subsumption under laws. Indeed, it appeared, laws are what have to be explained, rather than the primary explainers. The gas laws do not *explain* the behavior of gases. A *theory* of gases is needed, one that postulates an underlying structure of entities, relations, processes.[110]

So here, once again, something other than the product of induction, empirical laws, is needed if an adequate account is to be given of how explanation functions in science. And there is one further context where overreliance on induction also led to insuperable problems, as already noted, and that was in finding an effective way to distinguish between genuine laws and accidental generalizations. If all one has is empirical generalization, à la Hume, this crucial distinction hovers out of reach.

Part Four: And Finally to Retroduction

And so, at last, we arrive, by circuitous ways, at the account of inference towards which all of this has been tending. By now, its outlines should be moderately clear.

Beginnings: Let us return for a moment (only a moment!) to the seventeenth century. We left Bacon an inductivist but with a hint that this would not quite do. In Book II of the *New Organon*, he lays out a case-study in order to illustrate his new method. What is the nature of heat? He eventually concludes that it reduces to motion. But in the case of ordinary bodies, the motion of what? Bacon postulates minute particles whose constrained motion is responsible for the impression of heat when we feel a hot iron. But surely no inductive process of generalization could arrive at such a conclusion? Bacon's alchemical background leads him to emphasize the importance of "latent process" that "escapes the sense"; it is on this that the observed properties of things ultimately depend. An understanding of the "latent configurations" of "things infinitely small" is needed.[111] He never explicitly recognizes that the induction-by-generalization he has proposed in the opening aphorisms of the *New Organon* will not suffice to reach such configurations. He does, however, sketch a method of testing hypotheses,

laying the groundwork for a very different conception of science, one where hypothesis takes an
honored place, and the old ideal of demonstration
is finally laid aside. Bacon himself did not, however, envision this denouement. For him, science
still connoted certainty, though he must have sus-
pected that the configurations of "things infinitely
small" would not readily yield such a result.

The story of how this suspicion grew as the
century progressed is a fascinating one, too complex to follow here.[112] Descartes saw that hypothesis was the only way in which the motions and
sizes of the imperceptibly small corpuscles on
which the observable properties of things depend
could be reached, but hoped that certainty might
still be attained either by eliminating all alternative explanations save one, or by finding one
that fits the phenomena of nature so well "that it
would be an injustice to God" to believe that it
could be false.[113] Boyle more realistically set about
formulating the criteria to be used in evaluating or
comparing causal hypotheses, where the causes
are postulated, not directly observed. After an
acute analysis of the difficulties facing explanations that call upon imperceptible corpuscles,
Locke concluded that physics of the traditional
demonstrative sort is "forever out of reach", but
that the skillful use of analogy may still allow the

natural philosopher to attain the "twilight of probability".

Newton was misled by the quasi-demonstra-
tive form he had been able to impose upon his
mechanics into supposing that hypothesis could be
dispensed with in science proper. Though he himself made extensive and ingenious use of
unobservable entities of all sorts in the Queries
appended to the *Optics*, he believed he could construct a mechanics and a geometrical optics without their aid. (He was relying here on the
plasticity of his key concept, *force*: are forces
unobservable causal agencies, or are they merely
dispositions to move in a certain way?[114]) Because
of his enormous influence on those who came
after him, his restriction of science proper to two
modes of inference only, deduction and induction,
was to have negative repercussions for decades to
come, until the atoms and ether-vibrations of the
early nineteenth century once and for all showed
causal inference to underlying structure to be
indispensable to the work of the physical scientist.

This is much too rapid an excursion, but it
may give some hint, at least, of how long it took
the practitioners of the new natural sciences to
realize how powerful a tool their causal hypotheses could become, how far beyond the small world
of the human senses they could reach, and how
secure a knowledge they could ultimately yield,

despite their apparent logical fragility. This was just as surely a discovery as was that of the planet, Neptune, and like the latter, it was made in the first instance by the scientists themselves, not by philosophers reflecting on the quality of knowledge that scientists *ought* to aim at.

Whewell: The most perceptive nineteenth-century commentator on these issues was probably William Whewell, whose *Philosophy of the Inductive Science, Founded upon their History* (1840) made plain that only a detailed study of the actual history and practice of science could allow one to say how science is made.[115] Though he recognized, and indeed emphasized (against Mill) a third mode of inference in science besides deduction and empirical generalization, he applied the old label, 'induction', to it which may have obscured the importance of the point he was making. Induction for him is, first and foremost, an untidy inventing of hypotheses meant to "colligate", or bind together, the known facts and to reveal new ones. The first step is the crucial one of finding the appropriate "conceptions" that will enable the facts to fall together in an intelligible order. This is the distinctive contribution of *mind*, he notes, a contribution overlooked by the empiricists (a touch of *epagoge* still?).

But "induction" is not only invention, it is also verification. (In deduction and even to a large extent in induction, to discover *is* to verify; the fateful distinction between invention (discovery) and verification comes into view only when a third mode of inference is recognized.) A good hypothesis should explain the phenomena already observed, as well as predicting new kinds. Successful prediction is already a measure of truth. But when a "consilience of inductions" occurs, when hitherto unrelated areas of inquiry fall together under a single hypothesis, this can (he suggested) convince us of the truth of the hypothesis. Consilience involves, then, both enlargement of scope and simplification of structure. And it requires the scientist to follow the progress of a theory over time to assess whether its growth has been coherent or *ad hoc*.

Peirce: Peirce was the first to say straightforwardly that to deduction and induction, we must add a third (which he variously named abduction, hypothesis, retroduction) if we are to categorize properly what it is that makes science. Abduction is the move from evidence to hypothesis; it is "the provisional adoption of a [testable] hypothesis".[116] Unlike deduction and induction, it may involve new ideas and thus may require new language as one moves from known effect to unknown (and possibly unobservable) cause.

Unlike many of his contemporaries (Ernst Mach and William James, for example), he had no hesitation about inferring to unobservable entities. Criticizing James, for example, he notes that the sort of positivism which would question the propriety, in general, of such inference is clearly out of touch with the actual practice of physics. "Attempts to explain phenomenally given elements as products of deep-lying entities" (using molecules to explain heat is his example) are entirely legitimate; in fact, this phrase may be said to describe "as well as loose language can, the general character of scientific hypothesis".[117]

A number of questions immediately suggest themselves. Is abduction the *inventing* of the causal hypothesis, the hitting upon a plausible explanatory account? Or does it in some way involve the *evaluation* of the proposed explanation? In terms of a distinction later made famous in the philosophy of science, ought it be regarded as discovery or as verification? One does not need to ask this in the case of deduction and induction. But there seem to be at least two (or perhaps even a spectrum of) varieties of abduction, depending on how much stress one puts on the term, 'plausible', when defining it as a move from effect to "plausible" cause. Peirce gave more stress to the inventive side, raising the further question as to why this should be regarded as *inference*. "I

reckon it as a form of inference, however prob-
lematical the hypothesis may be held."[118]

There has been a good deal of controversy
among Peirce scholars as to how, exactly, in the
end he intended abduction to be understood.[119]
Some of this was prompted by the appearance of
N. R. Hanson's book, *Patterns of Discovery* in
1958,[120] since Hanson made use of Peirce's term,
'retroduction', in order to make his own point
about the manner in which discovery is "pat-
terned" in science. To "discover" a causal hypothesis is already to see certain phenomena as intelligible. He quotes Peirce with approval: "Abduction, although it is very little hampered by logical
rules, nevertheless is logical inference, asserting
its conclusion only problematically or conjectural-
ly, it is true, but nevertheless having a perfectly
definite logical form."[121] Hanson rejects the standard H-D account of causal inference, claiming
that (unlike the retroductive one) it leaves the
genesis of the hypothesis itself unaccounted for,
focussing only on the subsequent testing.

Peirce's views on the triad, deduction,
induction, retroduction, shifted in marked fashion
across the course of his long writing career. Early
on, he saw them as three more or less indepen-
dent types of inference. Later, he presents them as
three linked phases of the same inquiry, part of a
single complex method. Thus, induction in his ear-

lier account is more or less the sort of generalization across particulars that we have already
encountered in so many guises. It is basically a
sampling technique, yielding an empirical law.
Whereas in his later writings, induction becomes
the means by which abductive hypotheses are
tested, i.e., the final phase of inquiry. He is critical
of those who confuse abduction and induction,
regarding them as a single argument: "nothing has
so much contributed to present chaotic ideas of
the logic of science".[122] One (abduction) is prepar-
atory, the other (induction) is the concluding step.
They have in common that both lead to "the
acceptance of an hypothesis because observed
facts are such as would necessarily or probably
result as consequences of that hypothesis. But for
all that they are the opposite poles of reason."
The method of one is, in fact, the reverse of that
of the other. Abduction begins from the facts
without having any particular theory in view,
motivated only "by the feeling that a theory is
needed to explain the surprising facts". Induction,
on the other hand, begins from an hypothesis
already arrived at and seeks for facts to support
that hypothesis.

Whether, when induction is formulated in
this way, it *can* so easily be separated from the
prior stage of abduction is a matter of debate. In
what way, and to what extent, is background

knowledge to be taken into account in the original abduction?[123] Does abduction refer to the manner in which a hypothesis is constructed, or the manner in which a plausible hypothesis is selected from among the available alternatives? Are we asking: what hypothesis is more likely to be true, or: which one is more worth considering? Peirce himself had distinctive views on what he called the "economy of research" which led him to hold that one should ordinarily prefer the hypothesis that is more easily tested.[124] It is not easy to disentangle the theme of abduction/retroduction from the enormously complex and sometimes idiosyncratic metaphysical and psychological system Peirce labored to build and rebuild. In the closing paragraphs of this essay, we will leave this task aside to focus finally on a relatively simple statement of "the inference that makes science".

Proposal: The ambiguity we have noted above between the two "sides" of abduction can be dealt with, in part at least, by allowing that there are two quite different modalities to take into account. Let us restrict the term, 'abduction', to the process whereby initially plausible and testable causal hypotheses are formulated. This is inference only in the loosest sense, but the extensive discussions of the logic of discovery in the 1970's showed how far, indeed, it differs from mere guessing. The testing of such hypotheses is

of the most varied sort. It *does*, of course, involve
deduction in a central way, as consequences are
drawn and tried out. Some of these may be singular, others may be lawlike and hence involve
induction. But we shall *not* restrict induction to
the testing of causal hypotheses, as Peirce came to
do. Much of experimental science is inductive, in
the sense of seeking interesting correlations
between variables; all the factors are observable,
in the extended sense of 'observable' appropriate
to sophisticated instrumentation. (Aristotle's
restriction of the starting-point of natural science
to features that are observable by the human
senses has long since been set aside. Virtually
none of the properties on which such sciences as
physics and chemistry are built today can be perceived by us, one reason why the patterning
involved in perception is such a poor analogue for
scientific explanation.) Induction is *strictly* limited
to the observable domain. And it is only in a very
weak sense explanatory. Laws may explain singular occurrences, of the sort that the D-N model
was devised to handle. But these are the material
of history or of engineering, not of such natural
sciences as chemistry or physics. Laws are the
explananda; they are the questions, not the
answers.

To explain a law, one does not simply have recourse to a higher law from which the original law can be deduced. One calls instead upon a *theory*, using this term in a specific and restricted sense. Taking the observed regularity as effect, one seeks by abduction a causal hypothesis which will explain the regularity. To explain why a particular sort of thing acts in a particular way, one postulates an underlying structure of entities, processes, relationships, which would account for such a regularity. What is ampliative about this, what enables one to speak of this as a strong form of understanding, is that if successful, it opens up a domain that was previously unknown, or less known.

The causal inference here is therefore not the abduction alone, which is still a conjecture, even if a plausible conjecture. It is the entire process of abduction, deduction, observational testing, and whatever else goes into the complex procedure of theory appraisal. Recent philosophers of science have stressed that the virtues to be sought in a good theory do not reduce simply to getting the predictions right. One looks for "natural" explanations, for example, avoiding *ad hoc* moves even if these latter lead to correct predictions. One looks for "consilience", in Whewell's sense, involving both unification and simplification. This issue of the criteria of theory-appraisal is one of the most actively-discussed topics in current philosophy of science.[125]

Our concern here is not with the detail of this discussion. It is with the process of theoretical explanation generally, the process by means of which our world has been so vastly expanded. This is the kind of inference that makes science into the powerful instrument of discovery it has become. It allows us reach to the very small, the very distant in space, the very distant in past time, and above all to the very *different*. As a process of inference, it is not rule-governed as deduction is, nor regulated by technique as induction is. Its criteria, like coherence, empirical adequacy, fertility, are of a more oblique sort. They leave room for disagreement, sometimes long-lasting disagreement. Yet they also allow controversies to be adjudicated and eventually resolved.[126]

It is a complex, continuing, sort of inference, involving deduction, induction, and abduction. Abduction is generally prompted by an earlier induction (here we disagree with Peirce). The regularity revealed by the induction may or may not be surprising. Deductions are made in order that consequences may be tested, novel results obtained, consistency affirmed. The process *as a whole* is the inference by means of which we transcend the limits of the observed, even the instrumentally observed.

Let us agree to call the entire process retroduction. We are "led backwards" from effect to
cause, and arrive at an affirmation, not simply a
conjecture. Retroduction in this sense is more
than abduction. It is not simply the initial plausible guess. It is a *continuing* process that begins
with the first regularity to be explained or anom-
aly to be explained away. It includes the initial
abduction and the implicit estimate of plausibility
this requires. It includes the drawing of consequences, and the evaluation of the match between
those and the observed data, old or acquired in
the light of the hypothesis. Tentative in the first
abduction, gradually strengthening if consequences are verified, if anomalies are successfully
overcome, if hitherto disparate domains are uni-
fied, retroduction *is* the inference that in the
strongest sense "makes science".

The product of retroduction is *theory* or
causal explanation. It is distinct from empirical
law, the product of the simpler procedure of
induction. (This distinction is not entirely sharp,
since the language in which laws are expressed
and the procedures by which observations are
obtained are likely to be to some degree theory-
dependent.) The criticisms levelled against the
original Peircean account can be met, since the
claims of both "discovery" and "justification" are
recognized, and an implausible dichotomy

between them avoided. Even the original abduction with the modicum of assessment it requires (does the hypothesis, in fact, entail the data prompting its creation? is it testable? is it coherent with background knowledge?) can be called retroduction of a preliminary and tentative sort since it already gives some hint of what the cause may be. But, let it be emphasized again, retroduction is not an atemporal application of rule as deduction is. It is extended in time, and logically very complex. It *is* properly inference, since it enables one to move in thought from the observation of an effect to the affirmation, with greater or lesser degree of confidence, of the action of a cause of a (partially) expressed sort.

The language here is, of course, that of scientific realism. It is because the cause is, in some sense however qualified, affirmed *as* real cause, that retroduction functions as a distinct form of inference. Anti-realism reduces effectively to instrumentalism; whether the anti-realist believes that theories may in principle make truth-claims or not, if his or her view does not permit one, in practice, to make an existence claim of any kind for theoretical entities, the distinction between this view and instrumentalism is a distinction without a real difference. (Many of those who are currently called anti-realists are given that label only because they reject the standard arguments advanced in favor of realism. But most of these critics in practice affirm the existence of the same entities as realists do, with very similar qualifications; the difference is that they do not present arguments, even bad arguments, in support of their realism.)

The instrumentalist account of explanation reduces retroduction to a complicated form of induction, and theory to law. That is why in the positivist tradition the distinctions between retroduction and induction and between theory and law have been glossed over. If theoretical terms are, in effect, no more than devices used to improve the scope and accuracy of prediction, if "acceptance of a theory involves as belief only that it is empirically adequate" (i.e., predicts observable results correctly), in the influential form of anti-realism propounded by Bas van Fraassen,[127] then there really are only two sorts of inference after all. So that on the distinction we have been laboring to draw in these pages, much depends. It is not just a matter of logical convention. It is a question of the amplitude of our world.

Conclusion: It is a far cry from the demonstrations of Aristotle to the retroductions of modern theoretical science. Where they differ is, first, that retroduction makes no claim of necessity, and it settles for less, much less, than definitive truth. It can, under favorable conditions, when theories

are well-established, yield practical certainty.
Recent discussions of scientific realism show,
however, how hedged this assertion must be, since
the truth of a theory requires the existence of the
postulated cause under the description given in
the theory. Second, the inductions that
retroduction relies on are systematic and pro-
tracted, not simply a noticing of regularity. Third,
the observations from which retroduction begins
are, for the most part, performed by sophisticated
instruments; the limited scope and lack of precision of the human senses would never permit the
range of retroduction that is necessary if the
"invisible realm", as Newton called it, is to be
opened up. Fourth, abduction often requires the
introduction of new concepts and the testing of
new language. The necessity for this was not
appreciated as late as Newton's day; his Third
Rule of Reasoning postulated that the properties
of *all* bodies would be the same as those of bodies
accessible to the human senses, i.e., would be the
so-called primary properties, extension, mobility,
hardness, impenetrability, inertia. (He needed this
restriction, of course, in order that induction
might be, as he claimed, the all-sufficient method
of natural science.)[128] Central to retroduction, as
we know it, is the imaginative modification of
existing concepts or the creation of new ones quite
remote from the universals or forms that might be

abstracted from perceptual experience. Finally, though retroduction *is*, indeed, an act of the intellect, as the *epagoge* underlying demonstration was asserted to be, it is exceedingly complex, involving a whole series of discrete and well-defined operations, like the drawing and testing of consequences, the assessing of anomalies, and so forth. And it is open-ended; it continues for as long as the possibility of new and relevant evidence remains open. It does not terminate in an act of intuitive insight wherein one sees that the nature must be so.

Abduction would roughly correspond to the first part of the medieval *regressus* and deduction to the second. But abduction differs fundamentally from demonstration *quia* because it does *not* yield the certain starting point that demonstration *propter quid* requires. Induction, in turn, would roughly correspond to the intermediate phase of *investigatio*, but it is methodic and involves experiment and the measurement of properties inaccessible to the senses. Still, one can see something taking shape in the sixteenth-century attempts to forge not just a conception of science, but a method whereby it might be attained. The tripartite division gave an inkling, at least, of things to come.

What retroduction and demonstration have in common is the goal of causal explanation, the discovery of natures. Both are realist, one direct, the other much more guarded. Aristotle and Aquinas would marvel at the complexity of retroduction and the degree of invention it requires; they would be taken aback by the intricacies of structure that underlie the "simple" bodies of our experience. They would, doubtless, regret the inability of natural science to lay claim on "eternal and necessary truth", though Aquinas might not be altogether surprised at the news. But what they would see as their own is the goal of a progressive and well-founded understanding of the "natures" whose interlocking actions make our world what it is.

Notes

1. This familiar doctrine is found in the early chapters of the *Posterior Analytics*; see I, 2, 71b 19-22. I shall rely mainly on the standard Oxford translations (here that of G. R. G. Mure), with occasional modifications. G. E. R. Lloyd remarks that Aristotle "was the first not just in Greece, but so far as we know anywhere, explicitly to define demonstration in that way". See *Demystifying Mentalities*, Cambridge: Cambridge University Press, 1990, p. 74.

2. Three chapters in the *Posterior Analytics* (I, 18 and 31; II, 19) and two in the *Nicomachean Ethics* (VI, 3 and 6) are the main sources.

3. *Prior Analytics*, I, 30, 46a 17-21.

4. *Post. An.*, I, 18.

5. See, for example, *Prior An.*, II, 23, 68b 29; *Post. An.*, II, 7, 92a 37 – 92b 1, and especially *Post. An.*, I, 31, 88a 2-5, where he says that the "commensurate" or genuine universal requisite for demonstration can be elicited on the basis of frequent recurrence.

6. See Deborah K. W. Modrak, *Aristotle: The Power of Perception*, Chicago: University of Chicago Press, 1987, p. 175, and the references given there. See also D. W. Hamlyn, "Aristotelian *epagoge*", *Phronesis*, 21, 1976, 167-184.

7. *Post. An.*, II, 19, 100a 4-5.

8. Some have argued that *nous* is a separate capacity for intuition subsequent to the process of *epagoge* (construed as empirical generalization). We shall take it to refer to the state of knowledge brought about by *epagoge* itself. See J. Lester, "The meaning of *nous* in the *Posterior Analytics*", *Phronesis*, 18, 1973, 44-68, and Modrak, 171-6.

9. *Post. An.*, II, 19; 100b 14-17. G. E. L. Owen reminds us that there is a parallel account of *epagoge* in Aristotle's work also, where the starting-point is not perceptions but

endoxa, the common opinions on a particular subject. "Phainomena" in this account are not sense-appearances, but what appear to people generally to be the case. This sense of *epagoge* is linked with dialectic rather than with causal demonstration. See "Tithenai ta phainomena", in Suzanne Mansion ed., *Aristote et les problèmes de méthode*, Louvain: Nauwelaerts, 1961, 83-103.

10. *De Anima*, III, 4, 429a 14-17.

11. *De Anima*, II, 5, 430a 15.

12. *Metaphysics*, IV, 5, 1010b 1-3. The passage continues with examples of this sort of subjectivity: heaviness, for instance, will not be estimated in the same way by the weak and the strong.

13. *De Caelo*, III, 7, 306a 16-17. See Owen, "Tithenai ta phainomena", p. 90, and also Terry Irwin, *Aristotle's First Principles*, Oxford: Clarendon Press, 1988, pp. 33-34.

14. *Post. An.*, I, 31, 88a 11-17.

15. *Post. An.*, II, 11, 94b 27-30.

16. Indeed, he sometimes overlooks the (to us, obvious) possibility of bodies too small to be seen by us, as in his lengthy discussion of the nature and origin of semen in the different kinds of animals, and its role in generation (*Generation of Animals*, I, 17-23). His claim that in many species the male emits no semen would be an instance of this kind of oversight.

17. *Post. An.*, II, 14, 98a 16-19.

18. *On the Parts of Animals*, I, 5, 644b 25 - 645a 4.

19. *Part. Anim.*, I, 5, 644b 35.

20. *Post. An.*, I, 13, 78a 33-35.

21. *Post. An.*, I, 4, 73b 25-28.

22. *On the Heavens*, II, 8, 290a 16-24.

23. "Knowable" is better than "known" here. "Better known in itself" makes little sense: known to whom? Jonathan Barnes in the new Oxford translation (Oxford: Clarendon Press, 1975) renders the distinction by "more familiar in itself" and "more familiar to us". "Familiar in itself" is puzzling, since "familiar" makes essential reference to individual experience. Another way of expressing the distinction is found in *Post. An.*, I, 3, 72b 28-29: things "prior from our point of view" and things "simply prior".

24. *Post. An.*, I, 13, 78a 34-35.

25. *Post. An.*, I, 34, 89b 10.

26. See, for instance, Jonathan Barnes, "Aristotle's theory of demonstration", *Phronesis*, 14, 1969, 123-152, and William Wians, *Aristotle's Method in Biology*, Ph.D. dissertation, University of Notre Dame, Ann Arbor Microfilms, 1983.

27. See *Hist. Anim.*, I, 6, 490b 19-27, and *Gen. Anim.* II, 1, 732b 15. D. M. Balme gives an excellent review in "Aristotle's use of *differentiae* in biology", in Mansion ed., *Aristote*, 195-212.

28. *Part. Anim.*, III, 6.

29. "The formation of fat in the kidneys is the result of necessity, being, as explained, a consequence of the necessary conditions accompanying the possession of such organs." *Part. Anim.*, III, 9, 672a 13-5.

30. Allan Gotthelf attempts to answer this question positively in "First principles in Aristotle's *Parts of Animals*", in *Philosophical Issues in Aristotle's Biology*, ed. Allan Gotthelf and James G. Lennox, Cambridge: Cambridge University Press, 1987, 167-198. For a more skeptical response, see Lloyd, op. cit., p. 88, and "Aristotle's zoology and his metaphysics: The *status quaestionis*", in *Biologie logique et métaphysique chez Aristote*, ed. P. Pellegrin, Paris, forthcoming.

31. Lloyd, *Demystifying Mentalities*, p. 89.

32. *Meteorology*, I, 7, 344a 5-8.

33. *On the Heavens*, II, 5, 287b 34 – 288a 2.

34. A. C. Crombie, *Robert Grosseteste and the Origins of Experimental Science, 1100-1700*, Oxford: Clarendon, 1953, p. 290.

35. The *Posterior Analytics* first became available in the Latin West in a translation by James of Venice around 1140. But the obscurity of the text and the unattractiveness of its doctrine from the perspective of the prevailing Augustinian theology delayed its impact. See R. W. Southern, *Robert Grosseteste*, Oxford: Clarendon, 1986, 150-5.

36. Crombie, p. 84.

37. James McEvoy, *The Philosophy of Robert Grosseteste*, Oxford: Clarendon, 1982, p. 207. See his chapter 2: "Grosseteste's place in the history of science".

38. However, the "experimenta" or experiences he reports are for the most part culled from Greek or Arabic sources, and are rarely firsthand. See Bruce Eastwood, "Medieval empiricism: The case of Robert Grosseteste's optics", *Speculum*, 43, 1968, 306-321; "Robert Grosseteste's theory of the rainbow", *Arch. Intern. Hist. Sciences*, 19, 1966, 313-322.

39. This particular way of describing the effects of sin on the human cognitive powers was doubtless suggested by the famous description of the battle-rout in Aristotle's discussion of *epagoge* in *Post. An.* II, 19. Grosseteste disagrees with Aristotle, however, in allowing that God can illuminate our minds directly, so that in principle not all our knowledge need be based on perception. See Southern, pp. 164-9.

40. *Commentarius in Posteriorum Analyticorum Libros*, ed. Pietro Rossi, Firenze: Olschki, 1981, pp. 190-1. Grosseteste also remarks in this passage that the planets

are intrinsically brighter than the farther-off stars, a claim that could be fatal to Aristotle's attempt to make of this example a *propter quid* demonstration.

41. *Commentarius*, pp. 381-3; see *Post. An.* II, 16, 98a 16-9; *Part. Anim.*, III, 2, 662b 23 – 663a 17; III, 14, 674a 27 – 674b 14.

42. *Commentarius*, pp. 390-8. Crombie seems to be claiming in this passage that alternative causal theories have to be tested "by further observation or experiment" but it is hard to find this in the text.

43. S. H. Thomson, "The text of Grosseteste's *De cometis*", *Isis*, 19, 1933, 19-25, see p. 23; Crombie, pp. 88-90.

44. *Commentarius*, pp. 214-5; Crombie, pp. 74, 83.

45. Thomas Litt lists fifteen different places in his works where Aquinas refers, in one way or another, to the precession of the equinoxes, and no less than eleven passages where the system of Ptolemy is mentioned (*Les Corps Célestes dans l'Univers de S. Thomas d'Aquin*, Louvain: Publications Universitaires, 1963, chaps. 16 and 18). Aquinas was keenly aware of the differences between the Ptolemaic and the Aristotelian astronomical systems, and shows sympathy for both (p. 362).

46. For an extended discussion, see E. McMullin, "Matter as a principle", in *The Concept of Matter in Greek and Medieval Philosophy*, ed. E. McMullin, Notre Dame: University of Notre Dame Press, 1963, 173-217, especially section 2, "'Empirical' versus 'conceptual' analysis".

47. G. E. L. Owen, "Tithenai ta phainomena", p. 88. Owen is critical of attempts to read the *Physics* as empirical science, which to his mind necessarily makes it come out as "confused and cross-bred", p. 92.

48. For a recent comment, see John Jenkins, "Aquinas on the veracity of the intellect", *Journal of Philosophy*, 88, 1991, 623-632. I am indebted to my colleagues, John Jenkins, Eleanore Stump, Alasdair MacIntyre, and Fred

Freddoso, for discussions on this and related issues in
Aquinas scholarship.

49. *Summa Theologica,* I, q. 85, a. 5 ad 3 (Pegis translation,
slightly modified); see also, for example, q. 85, a. 6 c and
a. 8 c.; *De Veritate,* q. 1, a. 12 c.

50. *In Symbolorum Apostolorum Expositio,* in *Opuscula
Theologica,* ed. R. M. Spiazzi, Rome: Marietti, 1954, par.
864.

51. *De Veritate,* q. 10, a. 1 c.; see also ad 6.

52. Jacques Maritain, *The Degrees of Knowledge,* transl.
Gerald B. Phelan, New York: Scribner, 1959, p. 208.

53. *De Ente et Essentia,* c. 6.

54. *De Spiritualibus Creaturis,* a. 11 ad 3.

55. *De Veritate,* q. 4, a. 1 ad 8.

56. *Summa Theologica,* I, q. 29, a. 1 ad 3.

57. *Summa Theologica,* I, q. 29, a. 1, ad 3.

58. *Summa Theologica,* I, q. 85, a. 5, c. The distinction
implied here between the knowledge of *quiddity,* as the
initial rough apprehension of the "whatness", or dis-
tinctiveness, of a thing, and the knowledge of *essence,* as
the full understanding of the nature of the thing, is not
always maintained. More often Aquinas appears to use
the terms equivalently.

59. *In Boethium De Trinitate,* q. 6, a. 2 c. (Maurer translation). The reference is to *De Caelo,* III, 7, where
Aristotle does indeed affirm that the test of general principles in natural science (specifically in this case, regarding the manner in which mutual transformations of the
elements take place is consistent with sense-observation.
He criticizes his opponents' views on the grounds that
the principles they rely on lead to consequences that are
at odds with simple observation, and blames bias and
carelessness for their error (306 a 7-18). This passage is

compatible with either of two very different readings of Aristotle's point. One (the less likely) would be consequentialist: the warrant for a principle in natural science lies in part at least in the verification of the empirical consequences deductively derived from it; the other would still be "internalist": *epagoge* has to be *properly* performed (not disturbed e.g., by bias); if it is, the warrant of the principle is to lie in its self-evidence. Here, of course, lies the Great Divide!

60. *Summa Theologica*, I, q. 2, a. 3 c. and ad 2.

61. *Commentarius*, II, lect. 20, 14.

62. *Summa Theologica*, I, q. 29, a. 1 ad 3.

63. Alasdair MacIntyre, *First Principles, Final Ends and Contemporary Philosophical Issues*, Aquinas Lecture 1990, Milwaukee: Marquette University Press, pp. 24-7, 34-51. For an opposed view, see Melvin A. Glutz, *The Manner of Demonstrating in Natural Philosophy*, River Forest (Ill.): Pontifical Faculty of Philosophy, 1956. Glutz not only maintains that demonstration can be relatively easily arrived at, but that the Aristotelian-Thomistic notion of demonstration affords the proper model of proof for contemporary natural science.

64. MacIntyre, pp. 43-4.

65. MacIntyre, p. 38.

66. MacIntyre, p. 39.

67. MacIntyre, pp. 45-6.

68. MacIntyre, p. 44.

69. MacIntyre, pp. 35-6.

70. *In Boethium De Trinitate*, q. 6, a. 1 c.

71. *Commentary*, I, lect. 30; see also II, lect. 20.

72. "We judge of natural things as the sense reveals them"; in natural science, the sensible properties of a thing "adequately manifest its nature". *In Boethium De Trinitate*, q. 6, a. 2 c.

73. *In Boethium, ibid.* We can also proceed, he says, by simply affirming either transcendence or negation of sensible properties. He is following the lead here of Pseudo-Dionysius, *De Divinis Nominibus.*

74. *In Boethium*, q. 6, a. 3 c.

75. *In Boethium*, q. 6, a. 4 ad 2.

76. *In Boethium*, q. 6, a. 2 c.

77. J. H. Randall, "The development of scientific method in the School of Padua", *Journal of the History of Ideas*, 1, 1940, 177-206; partially reprinted in *The Roots of Scientific Thought*, ed. Philip P. Wiener and Aaron Noland, New York: Basic Books, 1957; see p. 146.

78. "Aquinas, Galileo, and Aristotle", Aquinas Medalist's Address, *Proceedings American Catholic Philosophical Association*, 57, 1983, 17-24; p. 22.

79. See W. A. Wallace, *Galileo and his Sources: The Heritage of the Collegio Romano in Galileo's Science*, Princeton: Princeton University Press, 1984; *Tractatus de Praecognitionibus et Praecognitis and Tractatio de Demonstratione*, transcribed by William F. Edwards, and with Introduction, Notes, and Commentary by W. A. Wallace, Padova: Antenore, 1988.

80. Nicholas Jardine, "Galileo's road to truth and the demonstrative regress", *Studies in the History and Philosophy of Science*, 7, 1976, 277-318; see p. 296.

81. Randall yields to the temptation, and presents the Paduan *regressus* as the immediate inspiration for seventeenth-century accounts of the "method of hypothesis". Thus, despite their both defending a strong continuity thesis, Randall and Wallace are entirely at odds as to

the *content* of what was supposedly transmitted to Galileo from Padua.

82. Jardine, p. 310.

83. Some of his uses of the term 'demonstration' in the context of mechanics are discussed in McMullin, "The conception of science in Galileo's work", in *New Perspectives on Galileo*, ed. Robert Butts and Joseph Pitt, Dordrecht: Reidel, 1978, 209-257; see 229-240.

84. These obstacles are of quite different sorts and the texts are not always easy to harmonize. See Mc Mullin, "Galilean idealization", *Studies in the History and Philosophy of Science*, 16, 1985, 247-273, and "Conception of science", pp. 230-5.

85. *Two New Sciences*, transl. Stillman Drake, Madison: University of Wisconsin Press, 1974, p. 153; *Opere*, 8, 197; see Mc Mullin, "Conception of Science", p. 229.

86. Wallace, *Galileo and his Sources*, p. 324.

87. Wallace, "Galileo's use of the Paduan *regressus* in his astronomical discoveries", to appear.

88. In a footnote, Wallace asks his critic whether he is certain (on the basis of pre-spacecraft evidence that the moon has mountains ("Galileo's use. . .", note 7). If not, "he must hold that planetary astronomy is not an apodictic science but only opinion, highly probable opinion, but opinion nonetheless". If he *is* certain, then he is committed to "a demonstrative *regressus*, whether he recognizes it under that name or not". This particular critic would respond that planetary astronomy is *not* an apodictic science, indeed that no natural science is apodictic, that the cut between the apodictic and the non-apodictic is not where science begins or ends. There are theoretical claims in every science which might loosely be called "apodictic" because of the degree of assurance with which we hold them. But the term is misleading because it tends to conceal the degree to which there may be assumptions hidden in such claims. Much better to acknowledge the presence of (highly supported) assump-

tions in quasi-apodictic claims on the one hand, and the value commonly attached to well-supported (though far from apodictic) theories on the other. Further, that someone should attach practical certainty to the claim that there are lunar mountains in no way implies that he or she has reached this by a *regressus* argument. A standard consequential argument can come to have such overwhelming force as to yield a (more or less) certain conclusion.

89. See W. Wallace, "Aristotle and Galileo: The uses of *hypothesis (suppositio)* in scientific reasoning", in *Studies in Aristotle*, ed. D. O'Meara, Washington: Catholic University of America Press, 1981, 47-77. For an opposing view, see Winifred Wisan "On argument *ex suppositione falsa*", *Studies in the History and Philosophy of Science*, 15, 1984, 227-236, and McMullin "Conception of science", pp. 234-7.

90. *Dialogue on Two Chief World Systems*, trans. Stillman Drake, Berkeley: University of California Press, 1953, p. 118; *Opere*, 7, 144.

91. These last claims are developed in some detail in McMullin, "Conceptions of Science in the Scientific Revolution", in *Reappraisals of the Scientific Revolution*, ed. David Lindberg and Robert Westman, Cambridge: Cambridge University Press, 1990, 27-92.

92. See E. L. Fortin and P. O'Neill, "The Condemnation of 1277", in *Philosophy in the Middle Ages*, ed. A. Hyman and J. J. Walsh, Indianapolis: Hackett, 1973, 540-9; Edward Grant, "The Condemnation of 1277, God's absolute power, and physical thought in the late Middle Ages", *Viator*, 10, 1979, 211-244.

93. See J. Reginald O'Donnell, "The philosophy of Nicholas of Autrecourt and his appraisal of Aristotle", *Medieval Studies*, 4, 1942, 97-125; Julius Weinberg, *Nicholaus of Autrecourt*, Princeton: Princeton University Press, 1948.

94. Francis Bacon, *New Organon*, transl. James Spedding, ed. Fulton Anderson, New York: Bobbs-Merrill, 1960, Bk. I, aphorism 19.

95. *New Organon*, II, aph. 2.

96. For a fuller discussion, see McMullin, "Francis Bacon: Exemplar of inductivism?" pp. 45-54 in "Conceptions of science in the Scientific Revolution"; Peter Urbach, *Francis Bacon's Philosophy of Science*, LaSalle (Ill.): Open Court, 1987.

97. *Novum Organon*, I, aph. 61.

98. *Preface to the New Organon*, Anderson, p. 36.

99. *New Organon*, I, aph. 50.

100. *New Organon*, II, aph. 36; see also II, aph. 7.

101. *Opticks*, Query 31, New York: Dover, 1952, p. 404. In his earlier work, Newton was much less guarded, and tended to insist, rather, on "deducing from the phenomena" as the mode of inference proper to "experimental philosophy". For a fuller discussion, see McMullin, "Newton: Deducing from the phenomena", in "Conceptions of science", pp. 67-74.

102. For a useful survey of the various formulations of Hume's problem, and a taxonomy of the many different solutions that have been proposed, see Max Black, "Induction", *The Encyclopedia of Philosophy*, ed. Paul Edwards, New York: Macmillan, 1967.

103. *A System of Logic*, 8th edition, New York, 1874, p. 223.

104. Rudolf Carnap, "The aim of inductive logic", in *Logic, Methodology and Philosophy of Science*, ed. Ernest Nagel, Patrick Suppe and Alfred Tarski, Stanford: Stanford University Press, 1962, 303-318; see pp. 303, 316.

105. A clear presentation of this approach can be found in the most popular textbook of the positivist era, Morris Cohen and Ernest Nagel, *An Introduction to Logic and Scientific Method*, New York: Harcourt, Brace, 1934.

106. C. G. Hempel, "The theoretician's dilemma", in *Aspects of Scientific Explanation*, New York: Free Press, 1965, 173-226; see pp. 184-5.

107. R. Carnap, *Philosophical Foundations of Physics*, New York: Basic Books, 1966, p. 230.

108. Carnap, *Philosophical Foundations*, chap. 24: "Correspondence Rules".

109. See, for example, Hempel, "The theoretician's dilemma".

110. See McMullin, "Structural explanation", *American Philosophical Quarterly*, 15, 1978, 139-147; Dudley Shapere, "Scientific theories and their domains", in *The Structure of Scientific Theories*, ed. Frederick Suppe, Urbana (Ill.): University of Illinois Press, 1977, 518-565.

111. *New Organon*, II, aphs. 5-8. See McMullin, "Conceptions of science", pp. 51-4.

112. See McMullin, "Conceptions of science", for a detailed account.

113. Descartes, *Principles of Philosophy*, part III, sect. 43.

114. McMullin, "Realism in the history of mechanics", to appear.

115. See Menachem Fisch, *William Whewell: Philosopher of Science*, Oxford: Clarendon, 1991; McMullin, "Philosophy of science, 1600-1900", in *Companion to the History of Modern Science*, ed. R. C. Olby et al., London: Routledge, 1990, 816-837.

116. C. S. Peirce, *Collected Papers*, vols. 1-6, ed. Charles Hartshorne and Paul Weiss; vols. 7-8 ed. by Arthur Burks, Cambridge (Mass.), 1931-5; 1958, vol. 1, par. 65.

117. *Collected Works*, 8, par. 60.

118. "Abduction, induction and deduction", *Collected Works*, 7, pars. 202-7.

119. See, for example, K. T. Fann, *Peirce's Theory of Abduction*, The Hague: Nijhoff, 1970.

120. N. R. Hanson, *Patterns of Discovery*, Cambridge: Cambridge University Press, 1958, see pp. 85-92.

121. *Collected Papers*, 5, par. 188.

122. "Abduction", *Collected Papers*, 7, par. 218-222; see par. 218 for this and the following quotations.

123. Peter Achinstein argues that the "retroductivist" account given by Peirce and Hanson does not square with examples drawn from the history of physics. See *Particles and Waves: Historical Essays in the Philosophy of Science*, New York: Oxford University Press, 1991, pp. 168-9; 235-9; 247-8.

124. For a detailed treatment of the manner in which Peirce's "economic" ideas influenced his theory of research, see W. Christopher Stewart, *Social and Economic Aspects of Charles Sanders Peirce's Conception of Science*, Ph.D. dissertation, University of Notre Dame, Ann Arbor Microfilms, 1992.

125. Thomas Kuhn's "Objectivity, value judgement, and theory choice" (collected in *The Essential Tension*, Chicago: University of Chicago Press, 1977, pp. 320-339) was in this respect a seminal essay. See, for example, McMullin, "Values in science", *PSA* 1982, ed. P. Asquith and T. Nickles, E. Lansing (Mich.): PSA, 3-25; McMullin, "Rhetoric and theory-choice in science", in *Persuading Science: The Art of Scientific Rhetoric*, ed. Marcello Pera and William Shea, Canton (Mass.): Science History, 1991, 55-76.

126. McMullin, "Scientific controversy and its termination", in *Scientific Controversies: Case Studies in the Resolution and Closure of Disputes*, ed. H. T. Engelhardt and A. Caplan, Cambridge: Cambridge University Press, 1987, 49-91.

127. Bas van Fraassen, *The Scientific Image*, Oxford: Clarendon, 1980, p. 12.

128. McMullin, *Newton on Matter and Activity*, Notre Dame: University of Notre Dame Press, 1978, chap. 1.

THE AQUINAS LECTURES
Published by the Marquette University Press
Milwaukee WI 53201-1881 USA

36. *Reason and Faith Revisited.* FRANCIS H. PARKER (1971)
0-87462-136-4

37. *Psyche and Cerebrum.* JOHN N. FINDLAY (1972)
0-87462-137-2

38. *The Problem of the Criterion.* RODERICK M. CHISHOLM (1973)
0-87462-138-0

39. *Man as Infinite Spirit.* JAMES H. ROBB (1974)
0-87462-139-9

40. *Aquinas to Whitehead: Seven Centuries of Metaphysics of Reli
gion.* CHARLES HARTSHORNE (1976)   0-87462-141-0

41. *The Problem of Evil.* ERROL E. HARRIS (1977)
0-87462-142-9

42. *The Catholic University and the Faith.* FRANCIS C. WADE,
S.J. (1978)   0-87462-143-7

43. *St. Thomas and Historicity.* ARMAND J. MAURER, C.S.B.
(1979)   0-87462-144-5

44. *Does God Have a Nature?* ALVIN PLANTINGA (1980)
0-87462-145-3

45. *Rhyme and Reason: St. Thomas and Modes of Discourse.* RALPH
MCINERNY (1981)   0-87462-148-8

46. *The Gift: Creation.* KENNETH L. SCHMITZ (1982)
0-87462-149-6

47. *How Philosophy Begins.* BEATRICE H. ZEDLER (1983)
0-87462-151-8

48. *The Reality of the Historical Past.* PAUL RICOEUR (1984)
0-87462-152-6

49. *Human Ends and Human Actions: An Exploration in St. Thomas' Treatment.* ALAN DONAGAN (1985)   0-87462-153-4

50. *Imagination and Metaphysics in St. Augustine.* ROBERT O'CONNELL, S.J. (1986)   0-87462-227-1

51. *Expectations of Immortality in Late Antiquity.* HILARY A. ARMSTRONG (1987)   0-87462-154-2

52. *The Self.* ANTHONY KENNY (1988)   0-87462-155-0

53. *The Nature of Philosophical Inquiry.* QUENTIN LAUER, S.J. (1989)   0-87562-156-9

54. *First Principles, Final Ends and Contemporary Philosophical Issues.* ALASDAIR MACINTYRE (1990)   0-87462-157-7

55. *Descartes among the Scholastics.* MARJORIE GRENE (1991)
0-87462-158-5

56. *The Inference That Makes Science.* ERNAN MCMULLIN (1992)
0-87462-159-3

57. *Person and Being.* W. NORRIS CLARKE, S.J. (1993)
0-87462-160-7

58. *Metaphysics and Culture.* LOUIS DUPRÉ (1994)
0-87462-161-5

59. *Mediæval Reactions to the Encounter between Faith and Reason.* JOHN F. WIPPEL (1995)   0-87462-162-3

60. *Paradoxes of Time in St. Augustine.* Roland Teske, S.J. (1996)
0-87462-163-1

The Annual St. Thomas Aquinas Lecture Series began at Marquette University in the Spring of 1937. Ideal for classroom use, library additions, or private collections, the Aquinas Series has received international acceptance by scholars, universities, and libraries. Hardbound in maroon cloth with gold stamped covers. Some reprints with soft covers. Complete set (60 titles) (ISBN 0-87462-150-X available at a 40% discount). Uniform style and price. New standing orders receive a 30% discount. Regular reprinting keeps all volumes available.

Ordering information:
Purchase orders, checks, and major credit cards accepted (Visa, Master Card, Discover, American Express).

Marquette University Press
Box 1881
Milwaukee WI 53201-1881

Phone: 414-288-1564
Fax: 414-288-3300

Credit card orders and other subscription communications may also be sent via the Internet to
TallonA@vms.csd.mu.edu
and via CompuServe email to Andy Tallon, 73627,1125.

Complete printed catalogue available on request. Catalogue also available online via the Marquette University web page, URL:
http://www.mu.edu/